STUTTHOF

Life and Death Under The SS

ANDREW SPARKE

APS BOOKS
Yorkshire

APS Books,
The Stables, Field Lane,
Aberford,
West Yorkshire,
LS25 3AE

APS Books is a subsidiary of
the APS Publications imprint

www.andrewsparke.com

First published worldwide by APS Books in 2023

FOREWORD

Two small boys are playing wargames as boys have done since time immemorial. They run towards the camera clutching guns made of wood, their knees grubby beneath the type of clothing in which small boys across Europe were commonly dressed for most of the twentieth century when out of school - shorts and hand-knitted, woollen jumpers. Nothing unusual about that…except that these boys are the two eldest sons of Max Pauly and the backdrop to their game is the Stutthof Concentration Camp where their father is Kommandant. What price innocence now?

PLACE NAMES

Given that the events described in this book chiefly relate to the period from 1939-1945 and to a concentration camp created by Germans in a country occupied by and claimed by them, the place names given throughout are those used contemporaneously by the occupying Germans although Polish equivalents are given in brackets wherever their addition might aid understanding of the text.

CURRENT LEGAL CONTEXT

With some justification, the Polish Parliament in 2018 outlawed as historical misrepresentation use of the phrases *Polish Death Camps* and *Polish Concentration Camps* since such camps, including Stutthof, were established and administered by the occupying German forces. Overall blame for the Holocaust does and should rest with the Nazis and Poland as an invaded nation had nearly 18% of its population - some 4.9 million people (3 million of them Jews) – murdered between 1939 and 1945.

More problematically though, the Polish legislation as drafted, and indeed subsequently enforced, has been deemed liable to blur historical truth regarding the assistance the Germans were given by some Poles in locating and arresting Jews living in Polish towns and villages. Furthermore within camps like Stutthof, some imprisoned Poles served as kapos or in other ways abused and oppressed fellow prisoners and this history of Stutthof necessarily contains examples of Polish collaboration, anti-Semitism and violence as well as of Polish heroism and altruism. The sad fact is that Poles cannot and should not be painted as universally heroic victims of Nazi oppression when the truth is far more complex and indeed human.

CONTENTS

INTRODUCTION

STUTTHOF has the peculiar honour of being the first concentration camp established on Polish soil. It predates Auschwitz-Birkenau, Treblinka and all the other places whose names became infamous as places of imprisonment or extermination for Jews, Roma, Sinti, Poles, communists, homosexuals, priests, trade unionists and illegally held prisoners of war.

German historical literature still makes the distinction, based on physical location, between German and Polish camps. To Poles such a designation is viewed as a gross insult; their country was subject to occupation by the Germans from 1939 and it was the invaders, with their need for slave labour and their *Final Solution* to the *Jewish problem*, who created the concentration camps, not the Poles on whose soil they were built. A further distinction is commonly drawn between concentration camps and extermination camps but that distinction could be seen as largely academic given the numbers who perished under Nazi camp regimes which showed no interest in the welfare of those incarcerated in them.

What is less widely appreciated is just how many camps there were acting as holding facilities or labour camps – over 1,200 across all the invaded territories. These were all de-facto death camps because they were founded to incorporate deliberate mal-nutrition and poor disease control as well as periodic bouts of group executions. Some of these are still maintained as museums and their advantage for visitors and researchers over places like Auschwitz is that the more human scale on which they operated is in many ways less numbing to contemplate but conversely more horrific because it relates not to unimaginable numbers of people but to individuals and groups who can be identified from the residual archives which escaped the German withdrawal from Poland in 1945.

One such concentration camp is Stutthof.

Stutthof is situated in the village of Sztutowo near Danzig (Gdańsk) on the Baltic coast of Poland and between 1939 and 1945 it took the lives of tens of thousands of the estimated 110,000 people imprisoned there.

This book has been written because there is not a great deal of material about Stutthof available in English and although copious Polish, German and Russian sources exist they are to some degree tainted by politically expedient inaccuracy and the physical evidence and archives do not entirely correspond with the hearsay evidence presented in post-war commissions of inquiry and trials. Atrocity propaganda was and is a residual issue particularly given Stalin's need to paint German atrocities as so much worse than anything perpetrated in the Russian gulags. However, Stutthof's story is horrific enough that it needs no exaggeration, only the bare truth, so far as it can be ascertained at this remove, to tell it.

PART 1
DANZIG

DURING THE HOT SUMMER days of August 1939, a series of twenty-one violent incidents took place involving assaults on German-owned property by supposed Polish soldiers and saboteurs. The provocations culminated on the night of the 31st of August with the Glewitz Incident. A German-owned radio station near Katowice was stormed, an anti-German message was broadcast in Polish and the attackers melted away, leaving some of their number dead from gunshot wounds to be displayed for the benefit of the world's press.

On the next day, the Reich Chancellor, Adolf Hitler, in a supposedly measured response to these Polish border incursions, declared war, and *Polenfeldzug*, the Polish campaign, was underway. Maybach tank engines were fired up and 2,750 Panzers began to roll over the border. One and a half million German soldiers were on the move with their tanks and horse drawn artillery as well as aerial support from Stuka dive-bombers in what would become known as *Blitzkreig* or lightning war.

Ten days earlier, on the 22nd of August, Hitler had promised his generals, in particular Fedor von Bock and Gerd von Rundstedt, commanders respectively of the frontline Army Groups North and South, a plausible excuse for war. "Its credibility doesn't matter. The victor will not be asked whether he told the truth," he said. He was in any event encouraged in his plans by the lack of any effective British or French reaction to his annexation of the Sudetenland or to the Polish annexation of Zaolzie (the western part of Silesia) in October 1938.

The radio station assault was carried out with military precision by men in Polish uniform. The men were in reality an SS unit led by Alfred Naujock, a twenty-seven-year old officer whose orders came directly from Rheinhard Heydrich and the Gestapo chief, Heinrich Müller. As part of the deception, a dead man was left near the open microphone with gunshot wounds. He was a fifty-three-year old German farmer, a Catholic Silesian with unfortunate Polish sympathies, called Franciszek Honiok. Arrested by the Gestapo the

day before, Honiok had been outfitted in military fashion, furnished with fake Polish army identity papers, transported to Gliwice, and there given a lethal injection, before his body, posed on the floor as a stage-managed exhibit, was finally shot, post-mortem.

The attack failed to deliver its planned outcomes. Gliwice was, it transpired, a relay station rather than a broadcasting station and the message fed by Naujock into the borrowed microphone did not override the main transmission and was not received by any of the audience awaiting the broadcast, including an irate Rheinhard Heydrich.

A further atrocity needed to be staged, this time in the shape of an attack on a German customs post. Murdered after that assault to add veracity were several more unfortunates, a handful of prisoners from Dachau, the Bavarian concentration camp established near Munich in 1933 to hold political prisoners They were killed in the same manner as Honiok and shot to create the illusion of a running gunfight with spurious Polish terrorists. To render identification impossible, their faces were horribly disfigured before the SS left the scene.

Sturmbannführer Naujock survived the war and his evidence, self-serving as it was - denying that he caused or knew in advance of Honiok's intended fated - established that all the incidents of supposed Polish provocation forming Hitler's pretext for mobilisation were *false flag*, German-on-German, missions carried out as part of the so-called *Operation Himmler.*

Polenfeldzug would last less than six weeks. It would all be over with Germany and Russia dividing the country between them by 6th October. Two hundred thousand Poles would be dead or wounded and nearly seven hundred thousand captured for the loss of some fifty thousand German troops. Long before then, the plans of two politicians in Danzig, hatched with fore-knowledge of the coming invasion and executed with dramatic haste on the very day the Germans were entering the country, created the first ever

concentration camp on foreign, non-German soil. The camp was not Auschwitz-Birkenau or one of the other infamous names from history but a smaller death factory on the Baltic coast and the men in question were the Senate President, Arthur Greiser and the city's Gauleiter, Albert Forster. The existence of Stutthof was in large part the result of their deadly rivalry for control of the Free City of Danzig and for recognition by Hitler and the higher echelons of the German Nazi Party.

Gyddanyzc was a natural harbour at the mouth of the Vistula river and wooden fortifications were built to protect it from the Tuetonic Knights during the mid-fourteenth century. A city gradually sprang up around the Wisloujście Fortress, attracting migrants from across Eastern Europe, not merely Poles, as it became an ever more prosperous port. Its prosperity proved an especially attractive lure for migrant merchants and settlers of German stock. As a polyglot city, the variations played on its name as the centuries passed demonstrate the ascendancy in particular eras of German or Polish interests; Gdanzc, Kdansk, Dantzk, Dantzig, Dantzigk, Dantzik, Danzig and finally modern day Gdańsk.

The Kingdom of Poland itself fared less well and ceased to exist late in the eighteenth century, its partitioned territories ending up in Prussian, Austrian and Russian hands but by 1914 Danzig had become one of the great shipbuilding centres of Europe as well as a vital exporter of coal and iron but the majority of its population were of German extraction and its official language was Deutsch. To all intents and purposes Danzig and its Silesian hinterland had become an irrevocable part of Greater Germany…and then the Germans and Austrians lost the Great War.

By the time the allied powers met to consider the demands which hardened into the eventual Treaty of Versailles, they were unified by a strong desire to lay all blame for the tragedies of 1914-1918 firmly on the shoulders of Kaiser Wilhelm and the German military, and to reflect their responsibility for the conflict in retributive reparations.

At the same time nations friendly to the allies pressed for the resolution of longstanding boundary issues and territorial ambitions, foremost among them the future security of the new, landlocked, Polish Republic brought into existence by a Polish nationalist proclamation in Warsaw on 3rd November 1918. The republic would require access to, or better yet control over, a seaport on the Baltic. That seaport was Danzig.

The new Polish state was surrounded by hostile and jealous neighbours, chief among them Germany and Russia. Its only apparently secure borders were those with Romania and Latvia. Now it was to gain a further tranche of German territory in Silesia, the so-called Polish corridor, linking the republic to the coast. The allies fought shy of delivering Danzig to the Poles as well and settled on a compromise satisfying neither Germany nor Poland. Danzig was to have a new status as a Free City, independent of both countries but with full usage of the port facilities guaranteed by the treaty for the Poles. In addition, the Poles were to control customs for all movements of people and goods in and out of Danzig. The scene was set for nearly twenty more years of hostility and provocation between the two countries until the deadlock was finally broken by Hitler's invasion on 1st September 1939.

Danzig's boundaries were laid down by Article 100 of the Treaty of Versailles. The new Free City-State which came into being in January 1920 comprised some 1,952 square kilometres and including the modern-day cities of Gdańsk and Sopot as well as Great Zulawy, the fertile coastal zone east of the Vistula extending beyond the villages of Stegna and Sztutowo on the Baltic coast. The Free City-State had Germany as its neighbour to the West and Poland to the south. It also had a serious issue because of its internal ethnic divisions. The city of Danzig and many of the surrounding towns and villages had a majority population of ethnic German extraction who regarded themselves as German rather than Polish and bitterly resented the formality of their separation from their motherland. The area also contained a sizeable minority of ethnic Poles who quickly found

themselves subjected to racial harassment and discrimination by their neighbours.

Poland was fully aware both of its vital need for deep-water harbour facilities on the Baltic Coast and that the solution endorsed by the Allied Powers was pre-destined to cause further conflict and as early as 1921, the Polish government sanctioned the building of a new port they could control at Gdynia, a few kilometres west of Danzig.

In 1933, Danzig fell under the administrative control of the local Nazi party and persecution of the minority Polish population became ever more overt. Polish Jews were particularly affected and an increasing Jewish exodus out of the region began. This was the time for Albert Forster and Arthur Greiser to tighten their grip upon Danzig to determine its future.

Arthur Greiser came originally from Posnan (Poznań). He was not an early recruit to the Nazi Party, joining the NSDAP only in 1929, with the membership number 166,635. Indeed, self-interest had first made him a Freemason, not a background likely to endear itself to Hitler. He was also a divorcee who conspicuously remarried in Danzig, a personal circumstance which constituted a political liability. To overcome the shadows of his past he needed to demonstrate fervent obedience to the Führer and he succeeded in doing this over a period of several years, rising to become Vice Chairman of the Danzig Senate. He must, accordingly, have entertained the expectation of succeeding Ernest Koch as Gauleiter of the city in 1930. He was to be disappointed.

Instead of a letter of appointment, Greiser received the news that Hitler was sending one of his favourites, Albert Forster to be the new Gauleiter in waiting. Greiser would have no choice but to work with and for Forster but theirs was to be a pragmatic partnership and neither seems to have liked the other from the outset. It would not be long before, behind a façade of unity, each would be endeavouring to sabotage the career of the other.

Albert Forster was a young, impatient, self-confident, impulsive and emotional Bavarian, qualities which quickly brought him to Hitler's attention after he joined the Nazi Party in 1923 at the age of twenty-one. When he married Gertrud Deetz in 1934, a marriage which may have been entered into to conceal homosexual tendencies, the wedding took place at the Chancellory in Berlin and the witnesses were Hitler and Rudolph Hess. Forster was only twenty-eight when he arrived in Danzig.

Forster's initial achievements were a dramatic expansion of NSDAP membership and taking control of both the city's Popular Assembly (the Volkstag) and its Senate. By the 1935 elections, he was using the same tactics of fraud and terrorism that had wiped out political opposition to the Nazis in Germany with the goal of achieving at least the two thirds majority which would enable the Nazis to change Danzig's constitution. To his distress he failed, getting only 59% of the vote, as much as anything because he had been unable to to solve Danzig's ever deepening economic crisis despite the devaluation of the gulden, Danzig's currency.

Thinking on his feet, Forster laid much of the blame for this dismal showing on his Deputy Gauleiter, the Vice Chairman of the Senate, Arthur Greiser and in consequence Forster's reputation in Berlin remained untarnished.

Even so Forster faced local opposition within his party which had not been cleansed of the influence of the SA (the *Sturm-Abteilung*), in the way that Hitler achieved in Germany with the arrest of Ernst Rohm and other leading brownshirt stormtroopers on the *Night of the Long Knives* - 30th June 1934.

Rather than having an SA favoured candidate thrust on him for the vacancy of President of the Senate occasioned by Hermann Rauschning's resignation, Forster found himself with little choice but to support Arthur Greiser's candidature although behind the scenes he emasculated the power Greiser would wield in the new role by placing his own civil servants in key posts serving the Senate such as

its Personnel Department. Even so by November 1935 Forster was at the centre of widely disseminated rumours that Greiser would be forced to resign for personal reasons.

Greiser, however, enjoyed one form of support that Forster did not. By virtue of their positions both held nominal rank in the SS but their attitudes to the city's *Schutz-Staffel* were markedly different. Greiser saw SS membership as an honour whilst as far as Forster was concerned his authority came from Hitler and the Party and wherever he found himself at odds with instructions from Himmler he ignored them, an approach periodically justified by the fact that Himmler's complaints to Hitler never resulted in any adverse consequences for Forster. There was no love lost between Forster and Himmler and Forster's contempt for Himmler's ethnic cleansing and Germanification of Poland resulted in a very succinct and personal criticism: *'If I looked like Himmler, I wouldn't talk about race.'*

In any event Forster wanted to exercise greater personal control over the SS in Danzig itself and to sever their regional loyalty to their divisional headquarters in Konigsberg.

Unsurprisingly Himmler, Hess, Joachim von Ribbentrop and Hermann Goring viewed Forster as a troublemaker and wherever possible supported Greiser even though Joseph Goebbels, taking his lead from the Führer, was strongly in Forster's camp.

Hitler's support for Forster or his disinclination to intervene in matters appertaining to the Nazi Party in Danzig left Forster's authority complete and unchallenged and the row between Himmler and Forster was never resolved despite Forster's regime earning negative comment from the influential SS Police Führer Richard Hildebrandt: *'I have never met with a Gau in which things are done so arbitrarily and with so little reason and sense.'*

External events were moving ever faster towards confrontation between Hitler and the Poles over the German desire to bring Danzig back into the Reich. On 4th July 1936 Greiser was to speak at the League of Nations about tensions over trade and customs duties and

the other flashpoints aggrieving the majority German population of Danzig. The text of the speech was personally approved by Hitler and Greiser delivered it well. At its conclusion he gave the Hitler salute, sparking laughter from the press gallery. Exiting the chamber Greiser thumbed his nose at the journalists. In some accounts he stuck his tongue out as well.

What Greiser had said and done played well in Danzig and he returned to a rapturous welcome. Meanwhile Forster lost no time in pointing out to the Führer that Greiser's conduct was a clear breach of Hitler's instruction that Nazi officials should behave in a dignified fashion when in the international eye.

In June 1938, Bishop Edward O'Rourke resigned as head of the Catholic Church in Danzig and with his departure, the last vocal opposition to Nazi policies in Danzig was gone. Forster redoubled his efforts to get Danzig to enact racial purity legislation mirroring the Nuremberg Laws adopted in Germany in 1935 and between 12th and 15th November 1938, Jewish shops, homes and synagogues were attacked in a direct imitation of *Kristallnacht* in Germany a few days earlier. On 23rd November the Senate finally passed their version of the Nuremberg laws and the push began to drive the remaining Jews, approximately 6,000 in number, out of Danzig altogether. Five hundred souls left for Palestine with police approval on 3rd March 1939 and *Kindertransport* evacuated many more children to Britain. By 1st September, the day of the German invasion, only 1700 Jews were left many of them older Danzigers destined for concentration camps, although a last group of 500 left the city by mass transportation in August 1940 heading for Palestine, which they finally reached in 1945 having been interned for the duration of the war in Mauritius.

If the so-called *Jewish problem* was well on the road to being resolved in Danzig by 1939, Forster could turn his attention to defending the city in the coming war. He approved the founding of *SS-Heimwehr-Danzig*, a home defence unit functioning as a part of the regular

German army structure and which oversaw the smuggling past Polish customs posts of armaments and military personnel.

Greiser meanwhile believed that he would be the ultimate beneficiary of Forster's efforts. He had been assured, presumably by Himmler, that Forster would be leaving Danzig to take up the post of German ambassador to Vienna and that Greiser would replace him as Gauleiter.

Then on 23rd August 1939 the Senate made Gauleiter Albert Forster, *Staatssoberhaupt*, a newly created position as head of state. Not far into the future that title would be converted by Hitler to *Reichsstatthalter*, effectively governor not only of Danzig but of the annexed Polish province of Pomerania (including the port of Gdynia) with its population of 1.5 million souls. He had won his long battle for supremacy over Arthur Greiser and it would be he to whom the honour of announcing Danzig's reunification with Germany would fall.

As for Greiser, he would move with most of his coterie of loyal Danzig officials to become Gauleiter of Warthegau where he would prove himself as brutal an exponent of Himmler's policy of Germanification of Poland as any other Nazi official. As Hitler said approvingly of him at the time of his appointment, '*He would liquidate the Polish intellectuals wherever he thought it justified.*' In other words he would cheerfully murder whoever stood in his way for the cause.

Another key figure in the story of Stutthof was Max Johann Pauly. The son of a hardware shop owner, Pauly was born in Wesselburen near the Danish border in 1907. His father died in 1928 and he took over running the family business, joining both the NSDAP (membership number 106204) and the SA in the same year. Two years later he married the daughter of a local cattle dealer and went on to have five children with her. In 1931 Pauly was, at the age of 24, an early recruit to the SS (his membership number was 5448) and he was a founder member of a new local SS branch, activity which gained him the rank of *Haupsturmführer*. In 1934 he underwent police

training and in 1936 was sent to Dachau with the rank of *Unterführer*, at which point he handed over the management of his hardware business to his younger brother. He showed obvious promise in the peculiar administrative disciplines required of Himmler's stalwarts and was earmarked for early promotion.

Pauly's next posting came through on 1st February 1937. His orders were to report to the Free City of Danzig as a secondee to the *Schutzpolizei* (Security Police). His brief was internal security and command of border guards and identity checkpoints. He performed those duties well and within months had risen to the rank of *Obersturmführer*. Allocated to a new unit formed in June or July 1939, *SS Wachsturmbahn-Eimann*, Pauly was allocated the task of finding a suitable location and commencing the planning for establishment of a prison camp to hold Polish intellectuals. The site he found was a clearing in the forest situated to the east of the coastal village of Sztutowo. In mid-August 1939, on Pauly's orders a group of a dozen or so prisoners from Danzig were taken there by the SS to fence in the clearing and erect some temporary structures for future use.

Plainly Forster, Greiser and Pauly were all in their different capacities preparing for a German invasion, or as they must have viewed it, liberation.

The battle for Danzig was a foregone conclusion, or so Gauleiter Forster, believed. Having taken the central railway station, the General Commissariat, the offices of Polish National Rail and the Polish secondary school without a shot fired, Forster proclaimed that as at 1st September the Free City had been re-incorporated into the Third Reich.

He was a trifle premature. With the German army still many kilometres away there were two remaining pockets of armed resistance in the city; the Polish Post Office, held by poorly armed but determined postal workers, and the Military Transit Depot on the Westerplatte peninsula, where around two hundred Poles were digging in to withstand the efforts of almost three thousand troops

and policemen supplemented by the armaments of the battleship, *SS Schleswig-Holstein.* Nevertheless, despite the crash of heavy ordinance and the chatter of machine gun fire, there could be little doubt that resistance to Nazi rule would be short-lived. Danzig would be completely subdued long before the German Invasion of Poland concluded but Forster would still have to wait seven days before it would be true that the city once more belonged, lock stock and barrel, to Germany.

The role of attacking the Westerplatte, and in the process firing the first shots of the Second World War, fell to Gustav Kleikamp. A Great War veteran, Kleikamp. had been promoted to the rank of *Kapitän zur See* in 1938. On 26th April 1939 at the age of 43 he was given command of an aging battleship, the *Schlesweig-Holstein.* He knew the ship well, having served a few years previously as its first officer.

The *Schleswig-Holstein* was a Deutschland-class, pre-Dreadnought era battleship built in Kiel and launched in 1906. She had twin turrets, fore and aft, housing her main armament, four 28 centimetre (11 inch) guns and she was also equipped with fourteen 17 centimetre guns. She saw action in 1916 in the battle of Jutland but was already outclassed by the new generation of British warships and found herself allocated mainly to training purposes between the wars.

In August 1939, Kleikamp received orders to sail to Danzig on a so-called friendship mission. but the true objectives were decidedly hostile. In a clear breach of the mandates governing the Free City which limited the Polish and German military to a nominal presence, the *Schlesweig-Holstein* carried a secret landing force of sixty men, six machine guns and four anti-aircraft guns and was reinforced by smaller vessels carrying a special unit, the 225 men of the *Marinestosstruppkompanie* which had been formed only the previous year and then deployed to occupy the Lithuanian city of Memel (*Klaipeda* or, in the Polish, *Klajpeda*). This was no friendship mission but an invasion force.

The *Schleswig Holstein* sailed into Danzig on 25th August and moored up on the Vistula opposite the Westerplatte. Kleikamp and his officers then took part in a commemorative event for the sailors of the *SMS Magdeburg*. The *Magdeburg* had run aground off the Estonian coast on 26th August 1914 and lost fifteen crewmen to shelling before she could be evacuated and destroyed.

Invasion orders for Poland were anticipated on the 26th but Hitler rescinded them at the last moment. The *Schleswig Holstein's* departure was then delayed because of supposed problems with refuelling and a Polish protest was lodged about her extended presence in the city.

At 04.47 on 1st September, after the invasion had been authorised by the German High Command, Kleikamp gave the order to open fire. In the next seven minutes, sixty-seven shells and some six hundred rounds of 20mm ammunition were directed at the Polish-held peninsula at a range of only six hundred yards. The effect seemed devastating. Wooden buildings disintegrated, barrels of fuel exploded, the ferry terminal and shipyard were flattened and the shockwaves dislodged roof tiles up and down the streets of the nearby Neufahrwasser (*Nowy Port*). It seemed improbable that anyone could have survived the naval onslaught.

Cessation of the shelling was the signal for the marines assisted by the soldiery of *SS-Heimwehr Danzig* to launch their assault. To their baffled astonishment they encountered stiff resistance. It was not only the Germans who had reinforced their military presence in defiance of terms of the Treaty of Versailles.

The permitted Polish military presence to guard the harbour was only eighty-eight men but, in the weeks before the German assault, the naval garrison's strength had swollen to two hundred and ten equipped with a field gun, two anti-tank guns, four mortars, and several medium machine guns. In preparation for a long-anticipated assault they had built reinforced concrete shelters in the basement of the barracks and carried out other defensive works.

A second frontal assault by ground troops on the Westerplatte, took place later the same morning and was repelled by noon. By now the original two hundred gallant Polish defenders were facing about three thousand German troops and marines reinforced by armed men from Danzig's *Schutzpolizei* (Protection Police), a force formed in 1921 but post-1933 firmly under the control of the Nazis.

A pattern was established of heavy shelling and dive-bombing by Stukas followed by infantry attack with the Westerplatte garrison emerging to return fire and drive off the Germans. What broke the defenders after seven days was simply lack of sleep and food and the mind-numbing intensity of being bombarded by a battleship at such close range. The Polish commander, Major Henryk Sucharski, apparently broke down on the third day, declaring his intention to surrender but was forcibly restrained by his junior officers from doing so. The fighting continued until the 7th September, when it was clear to all of them that no Polish military reserve was coming to their aid. The Polish garrison was allowed a dignified surrender ceremony with Major Sucharski offering up his sabre and General Friedrich-Georg Eberhardt graciously permitting him to retain it. Of the Poles on the Westerplatte, fifteen had been killed and over forty wounded. They had in turn killed about three hundred Germans.

The honour accorded to the gallant Poles turned out to be short-lived for some of them. The belated conscription immediately before the 1st September of the Westerplatte's civilian contract workers for the navy was treated as a sham by the Germans even if the individuals concerned were wearing elements of Polish uniform. These men were separated from those deemed actual prisoners of war (who could not lawfully under the Geneva Convention be put to work by their enemy) and were forced to serve as labourers tasked with clearing up the wreckage and debris left on the Westerplatte. When that work was done, those men were imprisoned at Stutthof. At the same time Polish wireless operator Kazimierz Rasiński was tortured and shot for refusing to reveal his military radio codes.

Together with the Westerplatte, the Polish Post Office headquarters, housed in the former Danzig garrison's hospital on Heveliusplatz, proved another thorny obstacle.

In April 1939, anticipating trouble, Army Reserve Sub-Lieutenant Konrad Guderski was detailed to Danzig to prepare the Polish Post Office for future hostilities. He proceeded to train forty-two local postal workers in the handling of small arms and to make the building more defensible by clearing the sight lines around the Post Office of potential cover like trees, as well as fortifying the entrance. In August, Guderski received ten reinforcements in the shape of post office employees from Gdynia and Bydgoszcz most of whom were army reservist NCOs. By then he had amassed a small arsenal of weapons - forty small arms, three light machine guns and three chests of hand grenades - with which he felt he might be able to fulfil the plan from the Polish High Command of holding out for the six hours it should take an army relief force to reach him. Clearly the plan envisaged an assault by local Nazi forces rather than an action ancillary to a full-scale German invasion which would render relief impossible.

On the morning of 1st September 1939, the Polish Post Office contained Guderski's fifty-two postal workers, the caretaker, a man named Barzychowski, his wife and their ten-year-old daughter, Erwina. At exactly 04.00 hours the telephone lines and electricity supply serving the Post Office were cut and the defenders stood to arms. Forty-seven minutes later the roar of the guns of the *Schleswig-Holstein* guns opening up on the Westerplatte provided the signal for a diversionary attack on the front entrance while the main force of police officers commanded by *Polizeioberst* Willi Bethke attempted to smash through the side wall, an assault supported by local SA units and troops drawn from *SS-Wachsturmbann Eimann* and *SS-Heimwehr Danzig* as well as three police armoured cars, one of them carrying Albert Forster who had come in person to view the fireworks. To complete the circus, local journalists had been tipped off and were in attendance to cover the action with a broadcaster from the *Reichssender Danzig* radio station and newsreel cameramen from *Ufa-Tonwache.*

What the bystanders did not witness was the immediate success Forster demanded. The attack did not proceed as planned. The diversionary assault initially seemed to have effected an unintended success with troops forcing the main entrance and getting inside the Post Office. However, trapped inside, volleys of gunfire killed two of the German attackers and wounded seven more, one of them the assault group's leader. Meanwhile the main attack managed to punch a hole in the wall but the soldiers were stopped by a grenade hurled by Guderski. What they did not know was that Guderski had been killed by his own blast.

The attackers retreated to confer with Bethke and Forster. The former strongly suggested the use of high explosive to blow up the Post Office and all its defenders but Forster was having none of it. He wanted to preserve the building for its propaganda value. Instead they waited for reinforcements which duly arrived in the form of two 75 mm artillery pieces and a 105 mm howitzer. It did them no good and a second offensive launched at 11.00 was repulsed.

Next mortars were deployed from the vicinity of the Westerplatte but their inaccuracy threatened to do more damage to the attackers than to the Post Office. By now it was 15.00 hours and the Germans called a two-hour ceasefire to enable the defenders to consider an invitation to surrender. During the ceasefire, German sappers undermined the Post Office and set in place a 600 kilogram bomb. It was set off at precisely 17.00 hours creating a breach quickly exploited by the Germans to seize control of the buildings, with the exception of the basement held by the Poles who still refused to surrender. At that point the only Polish dead were Guderski and two others.

To overcome the last remnants of resistance, Danzig firemen were ordered by Willi Bethke to pump all the gasoline from a railway tanker into the basement and that was ignited with a flame thrower. Three Poles were immolated in the resulting blaze and the others immediately surrendered.

The Post Office's director Dr Jan Michón lead the way out into daylight carrying a white flag with the Commandant, Józef Wąsik by his side. Both were shot on sight, although the Polish historians Cieslak and Biernat claim that Wąsik was burnt to death by a flame thrower.

All the other Poles leaving the burning building were taken into custody apart from six who managed to escape. Two of the escapees were picked up by the Germans in the days that followed and sixteen prisoners were hospitalised, six of them, including the unfortunate young Erwina Barzychowska, dying of their wounds.

Incarceration for the thirty-eight surviving Polish postal workers proved merely temporary. On 8th September they were put on trial as illegal civilian combatants before a military court set up by General Eberhardt and were sentenced to death. That sentence was carried out at about 04.00 hours on 5th October at the old training ground adjacent to Danzig Airport. The firing squad was commanded by *SS-Sturmbannführer* Max Pauly.

Following the capture of the Post Office and the Westerplatte, the fighting moved north away from the city onto the Hel peninsula where Polish forces held out until early October despite heavy offshore shelling from the repositioned *Schleswig-Holstein.* Among the surviving Poles who surrendered to the Germans was a Captain from Polish counter-intelligence, Antoni Kasztelan, one of many significant prisoners taken in the autumn of 1939 who would find themselves transferred to Stutthof.

Sometime before the German invasion of Poland, the Reich Criminal Police Department, (the *Reichkriminalpolizeiamt* or RKPA, also known as the *Kriminalpolizei* or Kripo for short and after September 1939 designated as Department V of the Reich Main Security Office) issued a classified document, the Special Wanted Book for Poland, *Sonderfahndungsbuch Polen.* It contained the names and personal information of around 8,800 Poles considered enemies of Germany due to their social or political affiliations and activities. All were

scheduled for immediate detention and most were arrested as planned during the autumn of 1939.

To the extent that the list of those marked for arrest in Danzig failed to correspond with Gauleiter Forster's prejudices, it was supplemented and the task of making the arrests was assigned to Danzig's Schutzpolizei and to the newly formed *SS-Wachsturmbann Eimann*, the unit named after its commander, Kurt Eimann, an *SS-Sturmbannführer* born in Görlitz in 1899. The official purpose of the unit was to provide security to the resort town of Zoppot (Supot) but its reputation swiftly became inextricably linked with acts of terror and repression.

An initial thirty arrests were made in the flats and apartments of Neufahrwasser on the Hinderstrasse (Kasztanowa Street) but to German frustration the searches unearthed no caches of weapons. Casting a wider net raised the number of arrests to one hundred and seventy. Virtually no resistance was offered although one Pole was killed and another wounded. More importantly, in terms of justification for the arrests, ten light machine guns and significant quantities of rifles, pistols and grenades were eventually seized.

Victoriaschule (the Victoria School) served as a temporary prison and an additional camp was created in Neufahrwasser since the most obvious site, the Westerplatte was still in Polish hands but on 2nd September a first batch of Polish prisoners was transported from the Victoriaschule to the construction site at Sztutowo.

There were plenty more arrests to come. *Sonderfahndungsbuch Polen* as a tool of Germanification postulated the rapid liquidation of the whole Polish intelligentsia and the nation's political, military and cultural leadership. To that end the initial purge was aimed at removing any Pole with higher education qualifications; politicians, teachers, police, lawyers, priests, officers in the armed forces whether serving or retired, bureaucrats and administrators, merchants and owners of businesses, doctors and veterinarians, writers and artists, and of course hereditary landowners.

After the fall of the Westerplatte, prisoners were immediately put to work clearing away the devastation on the peninsula and the *Schiesstange*, the prison at Kurkowa Street managed to accomodate eight hundred new prisoners. Many were early detainees first held at the Victoriaschule and comprised Polish railway and postal workers, customs officials and schoolchildren arrested across Danzig, but about four and a half thousand arrests were made in total and the detainees had to be imprisoned somewhere. The answer for some of them had already been determined in planning for the return of Danzig to German control; the creation of a prison modelled on concentration camp guidelines, the first such camp to be opened on non-German soil.

Not all the arrestees were destined for Stutthof, however. Some were earmarked for early execution. A few were subject to criminal trial and were duly hanged or guillotined in prison but a significant number of Polish prisoners were simply taken out into the Piasnica Woods in November 1939 to be shot. Other Poles rounded up by the notorious special units, the Einsatzgruppen following behind the advancing Whehrmacht were simply exterminated where they were found. It has been estimated that between September and December 1939 up to 60,000 political figures, landowners, clergymen, doctors and other members of the intelligentsia were murdered and even if that figure has been exaggerated, it must be the case that the actions of the Einsatzgruppen removed a huge number of Poles around whom resistance to German occupation might have gathered.

Danzig and Forster and Greisler played their part in this, unleashing SS-Wachsturmbann Eimann and giving Adolf Hitler their personal assurances as to the rapid Germanification of the region when he visited Danzig in triumph on 20th September 1939 and inspected the Westerplatte the following day.

By then the first prisoners at Stutthof had already survived eighteen nights under canvas and construction of the first Concentration Camp on Polish soil was proceeding apace.

Top Polish border control for Danzig at Gdynia-Kolibki
Bottom Police action in Danzig 1933

Nazi propaganda poster

Top Hitler reviewing the advance into Poland
Bottom German Panzers rolling into action

Fourteen-year old Polish girl killed in Luftwaffe strike

Assault on the Polish Post Office

SS-Wachsturmbann Eimann Rounding up the Post Office defenders

The Westerplatte

The Reich flag raised over The Westerplatte

German troops removing Polish civic insignia

From top left clockwise:
Greiser; Forster; Forster and Greiser with other Nazi officials

From top left clockwise::
Danzig policemen; Danzig Nazi officials; Arthur Greiser and his wife; German troops removing Polish signage in Danzig

SS-Wachsturmbann Eimann in operation

Clockwise from top left:
Kurt Eimann; Gustav Kleikamp; Max Pauly; Paul Werner Hoppe

Arthur Greiser in Poznan 1939

The Great Synagogue in Danzig destroyed by the Nazis 1939

Arrest of Polish Jews 1939

Hitler in Danzig and on Westerplatte 21st September 1939

The New York Times.

EXTRA

GERMAN ARMY ATTACKS POLAND; CITIES BOMBED, PORT BLOCKADED; DANZIG IS ACCEPTED INTO REICH

Hitler Tells the Reichstag 'Bomb Will Be Met by Bomb'

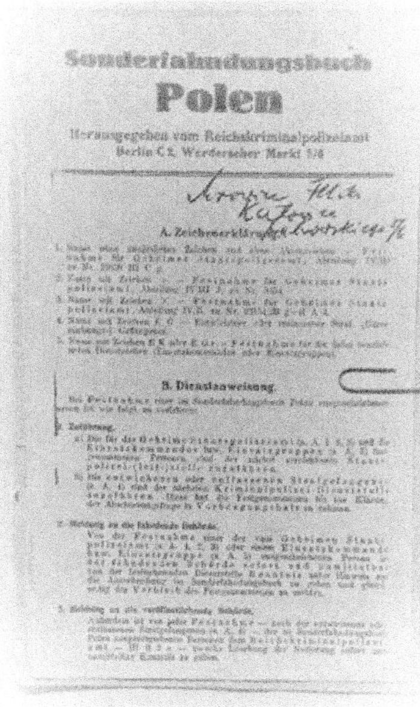

Sonderfahndungsbuch

Polen

Herausgegeben vom Reichskriminalpolizeiamt
Berlin C 2, Werderscher Markt 5/6

A. Zeichenerklärung

B. Dienstanweisung

Clockwise from top left
Front page New York Times 1st September 1939; Sonderfahndungsbuch Polen; Albert Forster (centre) at Dirschau, September 4th, 1940.

PART 2
CONSTRUCTION AND POPULATION

ON THE MORNING of 2nd September 1939, buses set off from Danzig to Stutthof carrying one hundred and fifty male Polish internees. Arriving at the site of the planned civilian internment camp, they found themselves standing behind barbed wire in a forest clearing some five thousand square metres in size. The only building on the side was the *Ostseebad*, a disused retirement home for the elderly which would be converted and extensively modernised into the camp's administrative hub, the Kommandantur.

The roughly cleared area contained a field kitchen, basic washing facilities and a latrine each sheltered beneath a wooden roof. This was the full extent of the work carried out in mid-August by the first work party, ten convicted criminals from Danzig under the supervision of *SS-Obersturmbannführer* Erich Gust (later to become a permanent member of Stutthof's staff) and his detachment from *SS-Wachsturmbahn Eimann.* They had however erected a dozen conical tents so it was obvious from the outset that sleeping arrangements would be cramped to say the least.

It must have been a shocking revelation to the prisoners of what lay in store for them. They were to be put to hard physical labour for which most of their lives up to that point had given them little or no preparation, fed minimal rations and crammed into inadequate tents overnight. They were given no proper work clothing and unless they had brought it with them, they would have to try to keep themselves clean without soap.

The work was back-breaking. They were required to cut down trees, clear stumps, dig trenches and foundations and carry building materials. The trees once cut down had to be transported to sawmills in the nearby village and when turned into beams and planks these needed to be carried back onto site where all the skilled work was carried out by the few craftsmen among the prisoners under the supervision of the *Technische Arbeitskolone.*

The scene at Stutthof was graphically described by Wlodzimierz Wnuk: ""To the sounds of striking axes and crashing trees, a huge

encampment is taking shape in the forest near the coast. Columns of emaciated men sag under the weight of bricks and iron bars, huge pine trunks cut into their shoulders, crushing them down to the ground. Encircled by barbed wire, a long row of barracks has grown out of the ground cleared by the sweat and toil of the prisoners. The barrels of machine-guns glitter where the frozen guards stand by, in the ice-bound world around even their breath forms icicles. Hovering above the camp are pulsating columns of smoke – as yet, still that normal smoke from burning wood."

At nights the internees were left to their own devices. Perimeter guards prevented escape but the rest of the SS officers and men were quartered outside the camp.

What was first constructed became known in time as the *Altes Lager* - the Old Camp, and it was situated on the edge of the village now known as Sztutowo, some 21 miles (34 kilometres) east of Danzig, near the Baltic sea and with a lovely beach close by not far from the popular holiday village of Stegna.

Driving through Sztutowo today, if the signposts for Stutthof did not exist, the traveller along the road out of town would see nothing of the camp other than the former Kommandant's house, a lovely villa property constructed for comfort, terraced at the front and with a view over open fields. The administrative heart of Stutthof, the brick built Kommandantur which also contained the living quarters of The SS guards, and the camp itself are tucked away in behind, among the trees.

The site of the camp is secluded and damp. But one thing is immediately apparent. It is not positioned in deep forest miles from anywhere but lies just off the main road, within walking distance of shops and houses

It is a reasonable surmise that there was no attempt to hide the camp or its purpose from the civilian population although in any event many were of German descent or were Mennonites, some of whom subsequently volunteered to serve at Stutthof.

The core elements of the Old Camp built in the first year at Stutthof were three parallel rows containing a total of ten wooden huts built on simple brick strip foundations and with a dirt floor. Each hut was sixty metres long and 12.5 metres wide with toilets and round concrete basins for washing in the middle although these were rendered largely redundant since the water supply was problematic and no soap was provided for inmates. Bunks were tiered three high almost touching the ceiling and the only other furniture each hut contained was a small iron stove for which no fuel was supplied.

The Old Camp as initially completed comprised eight barracks for prisoners, a workshop, stores, baths and the original infirmary plus the administrative buildings all painted battleship grey. Uninsulated and commonly lacking flooring, windows and doors the newly built structures offered little more protection for the inmates than the tents originally supplied. They were bakingly hot in summer - worsening endemic dehydration - and freezing in winter, a problem worsened by the lack of proper bedding.

According to the camps accounts, building Stutthof had by the end of March 1940, cost 299,459 *Reichsmarks* for a camp now having the capacity to hold several thousand inmates.

Later in September 1939, another transport of Polish inmates from Danzig arrived at Stutthof, this time a group of four hundred which contained a priest, Father Bronisław Komorowski from St. Stanislaus Church in Langfuhr and the curate from the new church of Christ the King, Franciszek Rogaczewski, the former President of the Central Committee of Catholics in Danzig. both arrested on 1st September.

A First World War veteran of the German army medical corps, Rogaczewski was forty-seven years old and survived less than four brutal months of beatings in Stutthof. His purported crime was storing weapons and preparing his church for active resistance against the Germans. Despite the personal attention of *SS-Untersturmführer* Otto Neubauer, Rogaczewski would not confess and he was among

twenty-two Poles shot by the SS just outside Stutthof on 11th January 1940 immediately after his return from a final interrogation at Neufahrwasser. Other victims that day included the priest of St. Piotr and Paweł in Wocław, Bernard Antoni Wiecki and Father Władysław Szymański

The fifty-year old Father Komorowski, who had been the only Polish member of Danzig's City Council of the city and served briefly as substitute in the Volkstag, lived only two months longer. Like Rogaczewski he was beaten until according to a camp survivor, Roman Chrzanowski, he was '…covered in blood [and] did not look like a human being.' Komorowski, together with a number of other Polish political activists, was taken into the woods near the camp on 22nd March 1940 and murdered. It was Good Friday.

One perhaps surprising fact is how few Jews were among the early inmates of Stutthof. Unlike Jewish communities within Germany, Danzig's Jewry seem to have had fewer illusions about the intentions of the NDSAP towards them. Not only did they send most of their children away on the *kindertransport* but took active steps before the German invasion to relocate themselves too. By 1939 only an estimated one thousand seven hundred Jews remained in Danzig and of those a mere five hundred were subsequently certified as fit, working age males. Those five hundred arrived at Stutthof on 17th September almost doubling the initial population of the camp. Despite their arrival Jews would not make up the majority of the camp population until much later in the camp's existence.

Poland never formally surrendered to either the German or Russian aggressors but hostilities became futile and ceased by 6th October. Six thousand Polish soldiers, many of them captured in Gdyina or on the Hel Peninsula, were then sent to Stutthof even though under the Geneva Convention they could not lawfully be forced to work for the enemy and should have gone to a proper Prisoner-Of-War camp rather than being interned with civilian prisoners.

The closure in November of a temporary camp at Grenzdorf established two months before to bring in the potato and beetroot harvests resulted in a further three hundred civilian internees being shipped to Stutthof. In the process the Nazi administrators learned the value of seconding labourers to satellite camps administered from Stutthof and shipping the workers back to their central camp when the labour requirement ceased or reduced.

The camp population thus grew within five weeks from one hundred and fifty to over seven thousand men - including evacuees from further away than just Danzig itself, as the Gestapo prisons in Torun, Bydgoszcz, Plock, Grudziadz and Elblag were emptied -and the building programme that entailed was already much larger than initially envisaged by the authorities in Danzig. It was the city's police which controlled the camp as a placed of incarceration for civil prisoners, a labour camp, the so-called *Sonderlager Stutthof* and thus it was the city itself which paid to construct and maintain the camp and provide the camp guards.

At that point Albert Forster and his cronies had no strategic plan beyond containment of those imprisoned there at the least possible cost to the city treasury. Even so according to the camp's accounts, building Stutthof had by the end of March 1940 cost 299,459 Reichsmarks.

The chain of command for Stutthof ran from SS-Sturbannführer Max Pauly through Kurt Eimann to the Danzig Police Praesidium. Pauly himself was not at first based at the camp because he had the Danzig prisons at the Victoriaschule and the Neufahrwasser barracks as well as the Grenzdorf farm camp to supervise and Neufahrwasser was the most convenient administrative centre for his geographically dispersed responsibilities. Only with the scaling down and closure of the other facilities and the removal of more prisoners to Stutthof did Pauly himself move to become the resident Kommandant.

Once ensconced at Stutthof, supervision of Pauly became sporadic. Gauleiter Forster had more important policy issues to manage in

Danzig and Kurt Eimann was too busy shooting people, often personally. In September 1939 *SS-Wachsturmbann-Eimann* was deployed in the former Polish corridor carrying out mass executions of Jews and by October were engaged with so-called mental defectives among Poles of German extraction – the *Volkdeutsch*. In all three thousand five hundred murders were attributed to Eimann's unit before it was disbanded in January 1940 and its members posted as reinforcements to the *SS-Totenkopf* division. Eimann himself survived the war, bluffed his way through Allied interrogations and and was never extradited to Poland to face trial for war crimes committed there. He was finally brought to trial at Hanover in 1968 but received a sentence of only four years imprisonment for shooting mentally ill patients and served only two years. His final whereabouts and date of death remain unknown.

Formal administrative procedures for Stutthof were in 1939 almost non-existent. Everything was being performed ad hoc. The prisoners, most of them with no recognised construction experience or skill, were building the imitial infrastructure for a camp of a size as yet indeterminate. There was no immediate numbering system for inmates arriving at Stutthof and when a register *(Einlieferungsbuch)* was established in October it contained around seven thousand names. Record-keeping was in its infancy and there were no uniforms or equipment save that which the new prisoners brought with them. Instead the inmates still wore their own civilian clothes, for the most part clothing not well-suited to surviving the wear and tear endemic in hard physical labour. Even once striped uniforms became available, they were not issued to the longest serving prisoners because they had no prison number and were in the main political detainees. All that happened was a requirement to paint a large red cross on the back of their increasingly tattered shirts, jackets and coats and on their trousers.

Under such conditions, civilised behaviour deteriorated rapidly. There was some attempt in the early months at cultural entertainment such as the Kashubian folk singing led by the conductor, Lubowmir

Szopinski but such planned events petered out as time went on and the demands of mere survival became more extreme.

There appears to have been no early appreciation in Danzig that the regime they had put in place for Stutthof must inevitably result in significantly more deaths than any traditional civil prison. Certainly, no facilities for handling corpses were built at the outset and the bodies of all those dying in the camp were initially sent away for burial or cremation.

Deaths there certainly were and not just from officially sanctioned executions. From the beginning the danger of punishment beatings from SS guards was present but the real enemy was the construction work itself. It was heavy and dangerous especially for exhausted and under-nourished prisoners and the energy expended on it was literally life-sapping because the rations allowed each prisoner were nowhere near sufficient to sustain human beings required to take part in even the lightest physical tasks.

Towards the end of 1940, a Summary Police Court met under the chairmanship of the head of Danzig's Gestapo, Dr. Helmut Tanzmann. A key panel member, given the task set them – to review the case of every current Stutthof inmate - was SS-Sturbannführer Max Pauly.

The case review concluded that 89 significant internees were incorrigable opponents of the Nazi state and that all of them - Polish officials, teachers, doctors and priests - should be executed. The sentences were duly carried out in the woods near Stutthof. Twenty-two men were shot on 11th January 1940 and another sixty-seven on 22nd March.

The court identified another 1,800 or so individuals for transfer to a properly designated concentration camp and these men were sent to KL Sachsenhausen in two transports on 9th and 19th April. Many of them were supposed associates of resistance movements, including members of the Command of the Defenders of Poland - *Komenda Obrońców Polski* and their friends and womenfolk.

Another 2,000 men, mainly Polish workers from Gdynia, were released from Stutthof towards the end of 1940 or in early 1941 to serve as slave labourers in Danzig's industrial concerns or neighbouring farms.

These changes left Stutthof with a reduced population of some 1,500 men (which presumably included the survivors of an initial group of about 450 Jews from Danzig who had arrived on 17th September 1939 – the only Jews who had not felt able to abandon the city before mid-1939) and the opportunity to plan for expansion of its physical footprint and the changes necessary to satisfy Himmler that the camp could and should be incorporated into the family of officially designated concentration camps with a wider role to play than simply housing the political detritus of Albert Forster's city and gau.

Camp construction continued throughout 1940. Prisoner labour was used to supplement the original barbed wire perimeter fence with guard towers at each corner and a depressingly impressive main gate, dubbed The Death Gate by the camp's inmates, outside which further wooden huts were built for SS administrative functions.

Other wooden structures built during 1940 included livestock barns and several hundred cages to support the breeding of rabbits for their fur rather than their meat.

Father Henryk Malak described the camp as he saw it on arrival as one of a group of Polish priests on 11th February 1940: "An enormous square was surrounded on the forest side by a high wire fence and to the right by low buildings of the 'house for the aged'. In front of us was a gate with barbed wire around it and beyond that – as far as the eye could see – a street with low wooden barracks on both sides."

The camp population now included scouts from Gdynia, Polish social workers, members of the underground resistance movements such as Gryf Pomorski and the Home Army and pupils from the Polish grammar school in Kwidzyn.

In 1941 a batch of professional German criminals was added to the mix and Russian prisoners of war began to arrive in 1941 after the commencement of Operation Barbarossa, the German invasion of Russia. Also sent to Stutthof were former members of the Lithuanian and Latvian governments supposedly as honorary prisoners. They were joined by a dozen or so Lithuanian intellectuals.

From January 1942 the camp was physically expanded dramatically with a brick-built *Kommandantur*, the headquarters for the SS guards replacing the old people's rest home which had been the only surviving original building on the Stutthof site. To the west of the camp, the Kommandant's personal villa was also built.

In September 1942 a company from Berlin was brought in to build two brick ovens and an 18-metre-high chimney. The first prisoner with the dubious honour of being cremated in the newly constructed ovens was the pharmacist, Stefan Kopczyński. However, a wooden roof over the ovens soon caught fire and early in 1943 a brick structure was built to function as a crematorium and a small gas chamber was added which was, initially at least, used to disinfect clothes for which Zyklon B (a hydrogen cyanide-based pesticide) was originally manufactured before the Nazis came to use it for gassing human beings. In fact no less an SS officer than the notorious Rudolph Höss, Kommandant of Auschwitz, would visit Stutthof to give instruction and guidance on the deadly use of Zyklon B in the Stutthof gas chamber.

From 1942 onward, prisoners of various nationalities were transferred to Stutthof from other camps like Mauthausen and Flossenburg and early in 1943 the new camp sited next to the *Altes Lager* was built behind an electrified barbed wire fence. It was to grow to contain thirty new barracks, twenty to accommodate prisoners and ten as armament workshops. The creation of the new camp coincided with the arrival of Ukrainian auxiliaries drafted in to work alongside SS guards.

In addition 1943, the camp saw a far more extensive system of satellite camps established primarily for Polish Jews but also for others from Czechoslovakia, Estonia, Latvia and elsewhere.

Then towards the end of 1943 a group of one hundred and fifty Danish communists and a number of German communists arrived at the camp.

The Gestapo in Danzig sent the first female prisoners to Stutthof in June 1940. Initially few in number they were accommodated in a hut to the left of the main gate but within months their number had topped a hundred and it became necessary to re-purpose one of the old camp's barracks blocks instead. The newly designated Women's Block contained Poles and Russians who were a mixture of re-education cases, and political, criminal and anti-social elements.

During 1941 a further 300 women arrived at Stutthof and thereafter the number rose incrementally to a few hundred by mid-1944.

Between August and November 1944 came a dramatic change; over 36,000 women were shipped in to be accommodated separately since they were mainly Jews.

Although not charged with the extermination of Jews from the ghettos of Eastern Europe, the camp population of Stutthof was to grow rapidly from 1943 necessitating further building and the expansion of the network of sub-camps (see below) to accommodate the rapid increase in the size of the available slave labour force and the overwhelming majority of the new arrivals were Jews.

The first wholly Jewish transports to Stutthof came during 1944 from Warsaw and Bialystok and then elsewhere in the occupied Baltic states being evacuated in the face of the advancing Red Army.

The major expansion occurred in 1944 when 75,000 prisoners, especially Hungarian and Polish Jews began to arrive en-masse from Riga, Kaunas, Konigsberg, Bialystok and Lublin. A large influx came with the evacuation of Kaiserwald in Latvia. These were primarily Jews from the liquidation of the Riga, Liepaia and Dvinsk ghettos

although there were possibly still some survivors of Kaiserwald's original population of ordinary German convicts. A great number of Jews were transferred on from Auschwitz whilst other inmates came from the Pawiak prison in Warsaw and from the evacuation camp at Pruszkow after the Home Army uprising of 1944. There were also transports of gypsies.

In all tens of thousands of people, perhaps more than 100,000, were deported to the Stutthof camp during 1944 and the arrival of masses of Hungarian, Greek and Czech Jews compelled the camp authorities to build a further ten barracks to the north of the New Camp.

By late 1944, Jews made up about 70 percent of the inmates and Russians another 20 percent. The age range had dropped too with the majority of inmates now much younger, with a disproportionate number of Jewish girls and young women.

The chaos and tremendous overcrowding arising from the mass transfers into Stutthof led to badly deteriorating conditions and an epidemic of typhus broke out and persisted during the second half of 1944. The death rate rose dramatically and reached a reported high point with nine percent of the total population dying that December.

Stutthof developed a large number of sub-camps (Außenlager) designated with the prefix AL to distinguish them from other geographically close camps not in common administration (Nebenlager) designated with the NL prefix. Some sub-camps were geographically distant from the main camp and their status referred primarily to their administration by the Kommandant of Stutthof since day to day oversight and interchange of slave labourers was obviously impractical.

The forty main satellites holding up to 110,000 prisoners from 25 countries were the sub-camps at Auerbach, Bottschin, Brodnica, Bromberg, Brusy, Chorabie, Cieszny. Danzig-Burggraben, Danzig-Neufahrwasser, Danziger-Werft, Dzimianen, Elbing (Elbag), Gdynia, Gerdenau, Graudenz, Grenzdorf, Grodno, Gutowo, Gwisdyn, Heiligenbeil, Jesau, Kokoschken, Kolkau, Krzemieniewo.

Lauenburg, Malken-Mierzynek. Nawitz, Niskie, Obrzycko, Politz, Praust, Pruszcz Schirkenpass, Schippenbeil, Seerappen, Slipski, Sophienwalde, Starogard and Torun (Thorn). Elbing and Torun were the largest of the sub-camps each holding 5,000 female Jewish labourers.

By 1944 the number of Stutthof sub-camps had grown to a total of 105 demonstrating the importance of Stutthof's slave labour to the German war effort.

One and a half kilometres from The New Camp a separate enclosure was created, the so-called Germanenlager to accommodate Norwegian policemen who had refused to co-operate with the Quisling government and from 1944 the 138 Finnish sailors interned in German ports following the signing of a peace agreement between Russia and Finland. In addition a special camp was built near the Germanenlager in 1944 to house a small number of new inmates it was deemed necessary to keep entirely separate from the rest of Stutthof's population. Apart from a dozen Hungarians, they were members of the German aristocracy and military with family members implicated in Von Stauffenberg's attempt on Hitler's life on July 20th 1944 as well as 150 Wehrmacht officers accused of collaborating with the Allies to secure a peaceful end to the war.

A manor house situated some four kilometres from the main camp at Stutthof, the *Gut Wederhof* was taken over by the SS in April 1942. The site contained both a farm and a brickworks and until January 1945, regualar work details marched there from the main camp every day mainly to see to the animals and perform other agricultural tasks.

As the situation deteriorated in the last few months of the war, from February to April 1945, the prisoners, who by then were all trusted Danes, Finns and Norwegians, were allocated a small house next to the manor and their tasks were to send as much food as possible, even rotten potatoes, to the main kitchen at Stutthof to enable soup to be made for the remaining inmates, many of whom were ill with Typhus.

In its lifetime Stutthof grew from 20 hectares to occupy a massive 120 hectares and had the war not been lost, plans were in place for still further expansion to give the main camp the capacity to house 100,000 inmates with yet more barrack blocks, a new hospital, more factory units and, most ominously of all, a larger crematorium. Stutthof would have become one of the largest Nazi camps in existence

However by mid-January 1945, there were an estimated 50,000 inmates of Stutthof about half of whom were in the main camp. And there were perhaps 29,000 Jewish internees, including nearly 26,000 women. These figures have however to be treated with some caution as accurate record-keeping was by now no longer such a priority.

Forced march evacuations towards the end of January 1945 brought the main camp population down to little more than 3,000 mainly sick inmates plus prisoners deemed essential to administering Stutthof while it still existed. The remaining prisoners were moved into the Old Camp, conveniently close to the Kommandantur, opening up the New Camp for use as a transit camp for up to 40,000 Wehrmach troops, forced labourers, POWs and German civilians fleeing the Riussian army.

Elsewhere forced march evacuations from Stutthof sub-camps and from Danzig failed to find safe havens and routes back towards Germany were being cut off by the advancing Red Army leaving their SS guards little option but to take them to Stutthof. Thus the main camp population grew again. By 27th March it had reached 5,148 - 2,811 men and 2,337 women, many of them isolated in the Jewish camp where Typhus was being allowed to rage uncontrolled.

The final evacuations by sea took place on 25th to 28th April after which the SS sought to burn the buildings holding the last Jewish hospital cases too sick to be moved.

The total number of prisoners held at Stutthof from 1939 to 1945 was something of the order of 110,000 people. Of those up to 30,000 died during a period of imprisonment in the main camp or the sub-

camps meaning the survival rate was about 70% despite the imposition of a numbingly brutal SS regime. However, the true death toll is likely to have been 60,000-65,000 once the camp evacuations of 1945 – the death marches and the Baltic Sea transportations – are taken into account because the survival rate for the evacuations was as low as 50%.

Arrests in Danzig 1939

Prisoners at Stutthof 1939

Construction work at Stutthof autumn 1939

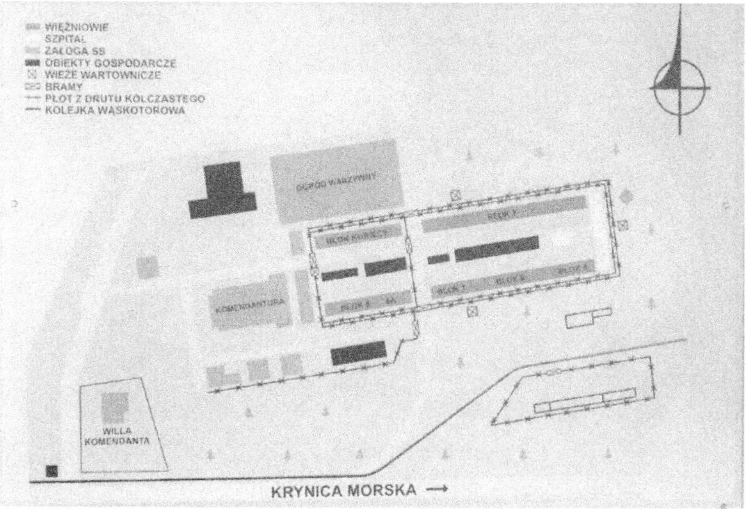
WIĘŹNIOWIE
SZPITAL
ZAŁOGA SS
OBIEKTY GOSPODARCZE
WIEŻE WARTOWNICZE
BRAMY
PŁOT Z DRUTU KOLCZASTEGO
KOLEJKA WĄSKOTOROWA
KOMENDANTURA
WILLA KOMENDANTA
KRYNICA MORSKA →

Gdyina arrests

Clearances Western Poland 1939

The kommandant's Villa at Stutthof

The Pauly family at Stutthof

The Kommandantur

The Altes Lager 1941

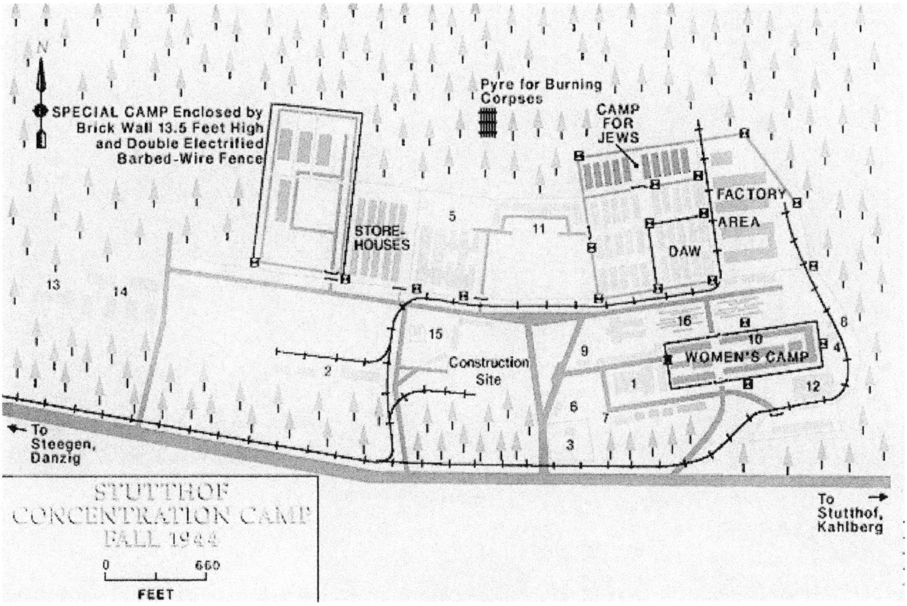

1 Camp administration block
2 Civilian workers barracks
3 Kommandant's villa
4 Crematorium
5 Disinfection & laundry
6 Dog kennels
7 Garage
8 Gas chamber
9 Guard house
10 Hospital
11 Planned new kitchen (never built)
12 Rabbit hutches
13 School for Ukrainian policemen
14 SS barracks
15 SS club-house
16 Vegetable garden

Factory units at New Camp

Gardens

Rabbit hutches and barns

Entrance to the Special Camp

PART 3
NAZI POLICY AND PRACTICE

VARIOUS STRANDS of Hitler's National Socialism led inevitably to the need to re-educate and control or imprison large numbers of German citizens and later those of the occupied territories.

Enemies of the Reich included Communists and later mainstream politicians and religious leaders as well as certain categories of criminal offenders, among them homosexuals.and as early as 1935, the Reich Minister of The Interior had formulated racial purity legislation which prohibited ethnically pure Germans entering into mixed marriages with Jews, regulations later interpreted as equally applicable to gypsies and negroes.

The perceived success of operations to euthanase the disabled and mentally ill gave rise to the monstrous ambition to cleanse Germany of all non-Aryan influences and in particular Jews and gypsies, for whom the so-called *Final Solution* became a process of mass transportation and murder which was also influenced the regime's treatment of Poles and Russians as ethnic groups deemed Untermensch, sub-humans.

The simple goals of re-educating recalcitrant ethnic Germans and eliminating opponents, Jews and gypsies, trialled with the establishment of the Dachau Concentraration Camp near Munich, later came up against a potentially conflicting requirement for slave labour to service German agriculture and industry once full-scale war was declared (see below).

Formed in 1923 as a personal guard for Adolf Hitler and comprising volunteers, the SS, as it had become by 1925, grew into a vast paramilitary organisation under the second Reichsführer-SS, Heinrich Himmler.

Himmler joined the SS in 1925 with the rank of Führer-SS and membership number 168. In 1929 he succeeded Erhard Heiden at the head of an organisation with 295 members which he persuaded Hitler to make independent of the Sturmabteilung (SA), the original

paramilitary wing of the Nazi Party. The ever ambitious Himmler then took every opportunity to expand the SS, using the perceived need to imprison and re-educate political opponents and to crack down on crimes against the state to build his role in policing until the SS secured primacy over all law and order formations. The SS encompassed what became the Deaths Head Units, the SS-Totenkopfverbände which administered and guarded the concentration and extermination camps, the Geheime Staatspolizei (the Gestapo - secret police), the Sicherheitsdienst (SD – the Nazi intelligence agency) and what later became a military division – the Waffen SS.

Invented by the British in South Africa during the Boer War, concentration camps – in German Konzentrationslager (KL) - became a particularly important tool of repression and social control in pre-war Germany. The first camp, Dachau was opened on 27th March 1933 by Himmler some two months after Adolf Hitler became German Chancellor. Its second Kommandant from June 1933, Theodor Eike, was at the time of Dachau's opening incarcerated in a mental hospital in Würzburg but Himmler offered him the chance to redeem himself and in so doing gained the eternal loyalty of the man who would go on to create the template for a vast network of camps for Himmler running a self-created Inspektion der Konzentrationslager (IKL).

The camps Eike created and oversaw would share a common architectural design - low barracks huts with rectangular assembly areas, surrounded by barbed wire fences with guard towers. They would not only look the same but would share a common ethos of punishment through terror despite a rule book that supposedly outlawed executions and physical violence by guards, even requiring Kommandants to secure permission from the IKL in Berlin for floggings. As is clear the rules were largely ignored since breaches seldom resulted in punishment.

Whilst there is copious available detail about what happened in the concentration camps operated within Germany and Nazi occupied countries up until 1945, the truth is that common understanding is partial and based on the assumption that concentration camps operated like Auschwitz-Birkenau which was in fact unique both in its scale of operations, perpetrating the deliberate genocide of one and a half million human beings and because with Majdanek (at Lublin) it had a duality of purpose. These two camps served as both labour and extermination camps, hence the separation of newly delivered inmates into those capable of work and those selected for immediate death. There was no need for such selections at Belzec, Chelmno, Sobibor or Treblinka. These were extermination centres and anybody sent there was under sentence of death. All the other camps were labour camps.

In all the Germans established some 1200 camps and sub-camps housing common German criminals, homosexuals, the mentally and physically disabled, Roma, Sinti, communists, priests, political opponents, dissidents and prisoners of war as well as the most numerically significant class of inmates, Jews.

There were eleven centralised concentration camps, providing slave labour and administering a vast network of subsidiary camps. These eleven camps were Buchenwald, Dachau, Dora-Mittelbau, Flossenbürg, Gross Rosen, Matthausen, Natzwester, Neuengamme, Ravensbruck, Sachsenhausen and Stutthof. Serving all the camps were two reception and holding centres, Bergen-Belsen and Theresienstadt. Some of these are notorious names whilst others seem almost unknown to the English-speaking world. Stutthof was not the least of the eleven main concentration camps and certainly not the small-scale camp which a visit to the remaining buildings preserved as a museum might suggest. About 110,000 people were incarcerated there during the six years of its existence and it lay at the heart of some forty satellite sub-camps.

If Auschwitz-Birkenau, Belzec, Chelmno, Sobibor and Treblinka were the camps charged with carrying out Hitler's Final Solution, the extermination of the Jews, the other camps existed to serve an altogether different policy - the provision of slave labour to profit the SS and to enable the Third Reich to win the war. Accordingly, executions required specific authorisation from Berlin. This is not to say that sadistic atrocities were not perpetrated by the SS and their kapos in these camps but they needed to be covered up in the administrative paperwork so that the records and death certificates stated false causes of death. This was necessary because needless killing deprived the state of essential labourers. Everyone entering the camps had to be accounted for and extensive records of prisoner arrivals and departures and deaths were maintained.

Oswald Pohl was a born administrator albeit one without a moral compass; a man able to work on the logistics of concentration camp management without sparing overmuch thought for the fact that the units and figures he was dealing with represented human beings and their suffering. The third most influential officer in the SS after Heinrich Himmler and Reinhardt Heydrich, Pohl was the man responsible for the transformation of the objectives of the concentration camps from incarceration and re-education to *extermination through labour.*

From 1938 Pohl had administrative and budgetary responsibilities for concentration camps and in 1942, with the rank of SS-Gruppenfuehrer he was promoted to head up the unified administration for the concentration camps and the Waffen-SS, the Wirtschafts und Verwaltungshauptamt (the WVHA or Main Economic and Administrative Office), a new department which also subsumed the inspectorate function for the camps. Pohl was a prime mover in the creation of the Deutscher Wirtschaftbetrieb (GmbH or German Industrial Concern) the role of which was to maximise the

profit generated for the SS by the exploitation of all available slave labour.

Pohl has been credited with the detailed calculations which assessed the value of the labour of a concentration camp inmate, given an average life expectancy of nine months, after deduction of the cost of food and clothing and cremation expenses plus the value of confiscated personal possessions (jewellery, watches, gold teeth and the like). The economic benefit of incarceration of an average inmate set by Pohl was 1,630 marks and it was success or failure to achieve this target which was to be a prime basis for evaluating the performance of concentration camp Kommandants.

Apart from setting the administrative and economic policies of the SS, Pohl had one more direct impact on Stutthof. Eventually he pushed Himmler to take away control of the camp from Danzig and bring it completely into the fold of the SS by granting it the formal status of a concentration camp.

This Himmler did in January 1942 and the former Sonderlager became officially a Konzentrationslager.

Pohl's arguments about economic management and the profits to be derived from better regulation of Stutthof's labour force were presumably the motivation for Himmler's decision. Up until then he had declined to change Stutthof's status, choosing instead to frustrate his ally Alfred Greiser's enemy Albert Forster who had been pushing for full integration of Stutthof into the concentration camp programme and regime, not least because the designation would remove the costs of managing and running the camp from the City of Danzig's budget and transfer them to the IKL in Berlin.

Fighting Hitler's war demanded considerable manpower, especially as the casualties mounted on the Russian front, as well as maintaining munitions manufacture, food production and logistical support. The answer lay in creating an immense slave labour system utilising the

millions of human beings being rounded up and sent to concentration camps. Stutthof and its eventual network of some 120 sub-camps was to become a major player in this market and as such a key contributer to the war effort.

The movement of slave labourers around Nazi-occupied territory and particularly the mass transportation of Jews from the ghettos of Eastern Europe was heavily dependant on the existence and smooth running of the rail system. Stutthof, for all its other advantages, had no direct standard gauge rail link. Instead it was served only by a few miles of local, narrow-gauge railway as far as the mainline station at Tiegenhof (Nowy Dwór) and the ferry crossing at Nickelswalde This immediately created a logistical problem because prisoners arriving from Danzig had to be sent by road and those coming from the east needed to be disembarked at Tiegenhof and re-embarked on narrow gauge cattle wagons. It may well be that this was one factor influencing the delay in granting Stutthof formal status as a concentration camp and it certainly precluded Stutthof ever being used as a mass extermination centre like Auschwitz.It is equally the case that products for the war effort manufactured at Stutthof required transportation by rail and thus the number of satellites and sub-camps remote from the main Stutthof camp but drawing their labourers from it multiplied to offer manufacturing locations with improved rail access.

The management of the concentration camp programme gave rise to a considerable and complex bureaucracy at SS headquarters in Oranienberg which had to be served by the camp administrations. The German desire for order and control combined with the comparatively low SS ranks of the senior personnel allocated to run the camps and the lack of clerical staff allocated to work for them inevitably meant heavy reliance on prisoners acting as the conduits for recording and maintaining data, allocating tasks and writing and submitting reports.

Thus Stutthof had to maintain SS personnel records, prisoner records, transport schedules in and out of the camp, transfer lists, death registers, labour allocations, files of orders from Berlin and Oranienberg, file copies of submitted reports both internal and those send to SS headquarters and files of the Kommandant's orders to staff, to name merely the most obvious.

Prisoner records were detailed, including date of birth and place of origin, allocated prisoner category and allocated camp number, physical description, next of kin, the work allocated and health records. Similarly detailed requirements applied to all other record-keeping.

To ensure records could be searched at will, accurate indexes were required. These included indexes of prisoners by both name and number, an index of prisoners with German nationality, and an index of deceased prisoners.

The Kommandant of every camp was required to report certain key information to Oranienberg on a weekly basis including numbers of prisoners held in each allocated category and numbers of Russian military personnel held. To preserve documentational clarity, no more than four carbon copies were permitted to be produced of such reports but Orianberg required five copies of the weekly report and since the camp needed to keep copies too, every report needed to be typed twice.

Bureaucratic interference didn't stop there. Non-German prisoner names, including Russian names, had to be recorded phonetically but Polish names did not. Corrections were not possible and therefore any initial typographic error must follow a prisoner for the rest of his or her incarceration. Births in the camp had to be recorded - whether occurring from women arriving in the camp already pregnant, from consensual, illicit, sexual encounters between prisoners, or rape or coerced sex with guards or kapos – but acceptable names for births to German women were prescribed. The mothers could not as a rule keep their children of course.

In a strange disconnect from the actuality of the behaviour of SS guards, the administrative regulation of concentration camps reserved flogging and corporal punishment to the express orders of the Kommandant; prisoners were not to be physically manhandled in any way. In Stutthof an Honour Code was signed by SS members stating that they would never strike a prisoner and undertook to report any breach of the code by another guard in the understanding that all infractions would be punished. In practice the code was breached every day of the camp's existence either directly or by ignoring infractions carried out by kapos and every officer from the Kommandant downwards could not be unaware of the fact.

Such was the administrative workload imposed on Kommanadants of concentration camps and Stutthof was set up to operate in the same way even though it was not awarded formal status as a concentration camp until January 1942 following a visit by Heinrich Himmler to the camp on November 23rd 1941. Until then it was a camp for civil prisoners, a labour camp, operating as the Sonderlager Stutthof and controlled by the police in Danzig. Concentration camp designation would, however, extend its functions, remove its funding from Danzig's accounts and lead to a wholesale change in its senior personnel.

Heinrich Himmler

Oswald Pohl on trial 1947

Theodore Eike

Himmler inspecting Russian Prisoners-of-War

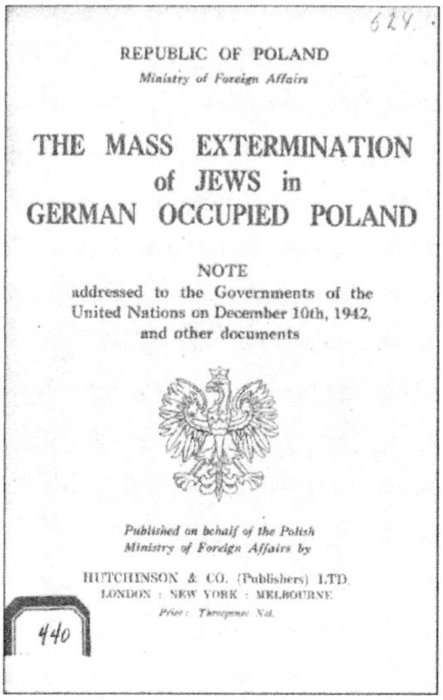

624.

REPUBLIC OF POLAND

Ministry of Foreign Affairs

THE MASS EXTERMINATION of JEWS in GERMAN OCCUPIED POLAND

NOTE

addressed to the Governments of the United Nations on December 10th, 1942, and other documents

Published on behalf of the Polish Ministry of Foreign Affairs by

HUTCHINSON & CO. (Publishers) LTD.
LONDON : NEW YORK : MELBOURNE

Price: Threepence Net.

440

Polish attempt 1942 to inform Allies of Nazi extermination policy

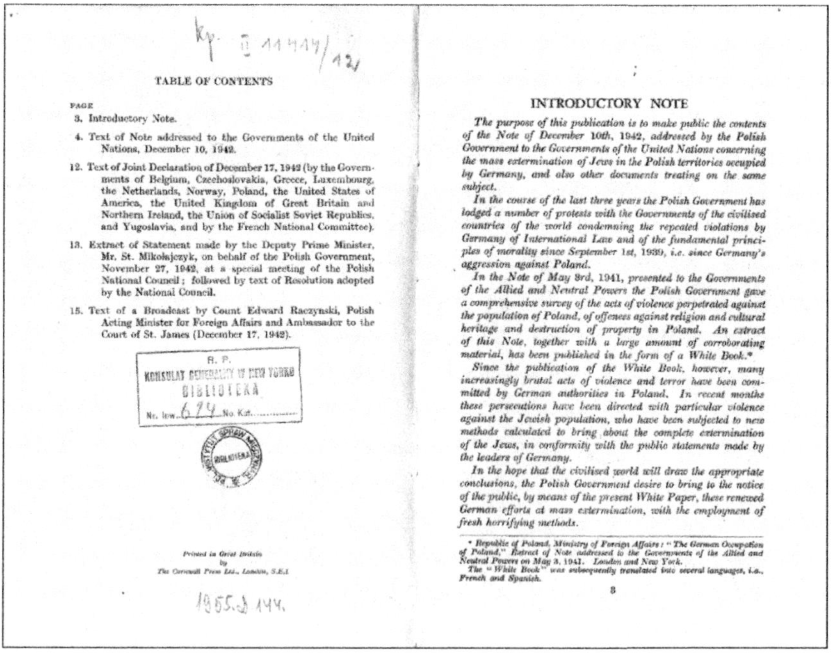

Ky. II 11 444/121

TABLE OF CONTENTS

PAGE

3. Introductory Note.

4. Text of Note addressed to the Governments of the United Nations, December 10, 1942.

12. Text of Joint Declaration of December 17, 1942 (by the Governments of Belgium, Czechoslovakia, Greece, Luxembourg, the Netherlands, Norway, Poland, the United States of America, the United Kingdom of Great Britain and Northern Ireland, the Union of Socialist Soviet Republics, and Yugoslavia, and by the French National Committee).

13. Extract of Statement made by the Deputy Prime Minister, Mr. St. Mikołajczyk, on behalf of the Polish Government, November 27, 1942, at a special meeting of the Polish National Council; followed by text of Resolution adopted by the National Council.

15. Text of a Broadcast by Count Edward Raczynski, Polish Acting Minister for Foreign Affairs and Ambassador to the Court of St. James (December 17, 1942).

R. P. KONSULAT GENERALNY W NEW YORKU BIBLIOTEKA Nr. Inw. 624 No. Kat. ....

BIBLIOTEKA

Printed in Great Britain by The Cornwall Press Ltd., London, S.E.1

1955.J 144.

INTRODUCTORY NOTE

The purpose of this publication is to make public the contents of the Note of December 10th, 1942, addressed by the Polish Government to the Governments of the United Nations concerning the mass extermination of Jews in the Polish territories occupied by Germany, and also other documents treating on the same subject.

In the course of the last three years the Polish Government has lodged a number of protests with the Governments of the civilised countries of the world condemning the repeated violations by Germany of International Law and of the fundamental principles of morality since September 1st, 1939, i.e. since Germany's aggression against Poland.

*In the Note of May 3rd, 1941, presented to the Governments of the Allied and Neutral Powers the Polish Government gave a comprehensive survey of the acts of violence perpetrated against the population of Poland, of offences against religion and cultural heritage and destruction of property in Poland. An extract of this Note, together with a large amount of corroborating material, has been published in the form of a White Book.**

Since the publication of the White Book, however, many increasingly brutal acts of violence and terror have been committed by German authorities in Poland. In recent months these persecutions have been directed with particular violence against the Jewish population, who have been subjected to new methods calculated to bring about the complete extermination of the Jews, in conformity with the public statements made by the leaders of Germany.

In the hope that the civilised world will draw the appropriate conclusions, the Polish Government desire to bring to the notice of the public, by means of the present White Paper, these renewed German efforts at mass extermination, with the employment of fresh horrifying methods.

* *Republic of Poland, Ministry of Foreign Affairs: "The German Occupation of Poland," Extract of Note addressed to the Governments of the Allied and Neutral Powers on May 3, 1941. London and New York. The "White Book" was subsequently translated into several languages, i.e., French and Spanish.*

3

Roma and Sinti deportations to Jewish ghettos

Forced labour in the Łódź ghetto

Liquidation of the Warsaw Ghetto 1944

PART 4
INMATES AND VICTIMS

IF THE PHYSICAL structures created at Stutthof can be regarded as an entirely recognisable replication of the existing Nazi concentration camps in Germany, the same cannot be said of Stutthof's imprisoned population which formed an atypical melting pot of races and backgrounds.

The original civil camp, the Sonderlager housed criminals from Danzig, often ethnically German, some of them common thieves, swindlers and murderers while others had fallen foul of the miscegenation laws precluding sexual relations with and marriage to Jewesses. The camp also contained Polish combatants and other Poles whose names appeared in the *Sonderfahndungsbuch Polen,* priests from across Eastern Europe and the last remnant of working age Jews who had failed to flee from Danzig before the summer of 1939,

Later as a designated Concentration Camp, Stutthof also housed Russian and Hungarian prisoners-of-war, Scandanavians (Danes, Norwegians and Finns), Latvian resistance fighters and assorted British, French, Czech, Dutch, Belgian, Latvian, Lithuanian, Belarusian and Croatian prisoners. The registered inmates also included a number of psychiatric patients.

The age range of these disparate internees commonly fell between 14 and 65. The camp was intended from its early days to contain those expected to labour for the Third Reich and so small children were rare and it was equally devoid of old people who were more likely to be transported elsewhere if not eliminated directly by the *Einsatzgruppen* or gassed elsewhere after 1943.

The original inmates of Stutthof also shared one other characteristic – they were all male. This was largely the case until 1941 when a proper women's barracks was established within Stutthof's existing compounds. Another factor which renders Stutthof different from other camps established in Poland is that until quite late in its history Jews formed a minority among the inmates.

The Geneva Convention of 1929 as ratified by Germany in 1934 clearly states that enemy combatants captured in uniform can only be

held as prisoners-of-war in appropriate and sanitary facilities akin to the barracks used by their captors, cannot be denied food of similar quality and quantity to their captors, and cannot be required to carry out war-related work. From the onset of the Second World War, the Germans chose to ignore the Convention whenever it suited them to do so and there were between 1939 and 1945 copious examples of flagrant breaches with captured personnel being summarily shot, interrogated and tortured for information and forced to work as slave labourers. The treatment of surrendering Polish military personnel affords more than its fair share of such POW. abuse. Many officers were of course ultimately clandestinely executed as part of the German plans to remove the upper tiers of subjugated Polish society. The same treatment was of course meted out to all captured Russian commissars and Political Officers. Other Polish military personnel were treated as though they were civilian criminals and sent to be held at Stutthof among them some of the defenders of the Hel Peninsula.

One such arrestee was Captain Antoni Kasztelan.

Alongside Commander Marian Majewski, Captain Kasztelan negotiated the surrender of local Polish forces at the Grand Hotel in Zoppot (Sopot) with the Wehrmacht commander in the Gulf of Danzig, Leonard Kaupisch. As a uniformed naval officer taking part in the defence of the Hel Peninsula, he should then have been interned for the duration of the war. Instead in November 1939 he was handed over to the Gestapo in Danzig.

Kasztelan was a brave man who stubbornly resisted the initial efforts of his interrogators to tap the knowledge in his head and brutal attempts were made to crack his resistance. Kasztelan's value lay in the military duties he had performed as Head of Counterintelligence in the Coastal Defence Command before the German invasion. The extent to which the captain was able to defy his captors despite being tortured led to a spiteful revenge – ultimately, he was put on trial and sentenced to death.

On the 4th February 4, 1941, Kasztelan found himself in Stutthof concentration camp (as prisoner 10433) where he was to remain until the end of the year. During his time in the camp he helped organise an underground resistance movement committed to sabotage and making the lives of the SS guards more difficult.

Given the energy and ingenuity allied to his military training, it must have come as some relief to the Germans when orders came to transfer him back to Danzig. There on 12th January 1942 he was brought before a special court and sentenced to death for *acting to the detriment of the German state.* He was executed by guillotine at Krolewiec Prison on 14th December, the punishment reserved for criminals rather than the firing squad he might have anticipated as a Polish officer.

Kasztelan was not the the only Polish intelligence and counter-espionage officer to be sifted out of the normal POW process, interrogated by the Gestapo and then imprisoned in Stutthof. Among his companions were three other young naval officers; Lieutenant Franciszek Sokół and Sub-Lieutenants Kazimierz Rusinek and Franciszek Herber. A number of other members of the Polish armed forces were also at Stutthof including the pilot Wacław Jurek and two army officers, Rudolf Ostrihansky and Ryszard Szymanik, all of whom survived the camp.

The majority of the inmate population until the end of 1940, comprised Poles but their places of origin and capture were far more widespread than the boundaries of the former Free City-State of Danzig. They included employees from Gdyina's Maritime Academy, three hundred Pomeranian priests and two hundred civilians from Torun and Bydgoszcz as well as teachers and pupils from the Polish Gymnasium in Marienwerder who had been transferred from Hohenbruch near Konigsberg. They included Boy Scouts and former civilan employees of the navy who had helped defend the Westerplatte.

Danzig's pre-war population was pre-dominantly German and thus a large proportion of the prisoners convicted before 1939 were of German ancestry. Given the callous dehumanisation endemic in the concentration camp regime in which inmates were in the main regarded by the SS as *Untermensch*, racially inferior, criminals of German origin possessed a unique survival advantage. They were individuals with whom their guards had most in common. Thus they tended to be better treated and a number became trustees or kapos, enforcing prisoner discipline for their masters. Some evidenced cruelty towards their charges at least as bad as the SS guards.

Stutthof would during its existence hold a number of such thieves, murderers and swindlers of both German and lower class Polish descent but not all those labelled as criminals held in Stutthof would ordinarily meet the definition of that term. One such was a resident of Elbing called Erich Wolf. He was sent to Stutthof on 21st October 1943 for breaching the Law For The Protection of German Blood by having intimate relations with a German woman. Others were supposed malingerers who had failed to report to Danzig's Ministry of Labour or absconded from their allocated duties.

Among the criminals imprisoned indefinitely at Stutthof were lesser criminals including pimps and later, once a women's barracks was established, prostitutes, each serving a fifty-six day sentence with hard labour, which could be repeated until the offender's re-education was deemed complete. At that point they could be released upon signing an affirmation that they had been well-treated at Stutthof but were left in no doubt that their behaviour on returning to their hometown would be monitored and they could be shipped back to the camp without further warning.

Mention has already been made of the first Polish priests to be imprisoned at Stutthof and executed in the autumn of 1939. More Polish priests were taken there in 1940.

Father Henry Malak arrived at Stutthof on 11th February 1940. He and a group of fellow priests were driven in a bus with the windows

blacked out from Świecie to Danzig the day before and then transported on to the camp in open trucks, arriving chilled to the bone and with their clothes rimed in frost. They were met by SS-Rottenführer Richard Akolt who alarmed them considerably with what he told them but as they were to learn in due course Akolt, older than most of his SS colleagues was to prove one of the gentler guards which presumably explains the light prison sentence he would receive in 1946.

Also greeting the new arrivals were a bunch of skeletal men dressed in rags who Malak was horrified to discover were fellow priests, some of whom had been in the camp for no more than two months but whose physical health had been destroyed in that short time.

Malak was at Stutthof for less than two months. On 9th April 1940 he was sent as one of 200 younger priests on a forced march to the station at Tiegenhof (Nowy Dwór) and then shipped by train to Sachsenhausen. Few of Malak's companions survived the war and indeed the events of 22nd March must have made any doubters realise that the Germans fully intended to eliminate all of them over time. On that morning forty of the younger priests including Malak were marched into the woods where they were forced to level a track for use by heavy trucks. When the task was complete they had to lie down and on pain of being shot themselves were ordered not to watch. Several well laden trucks duly passed and then the work party was marched back to camp. There they discovered that all the living Polish intellectuals and the older priests including Father Górecki and Father Komorowski had gone. The trucks had carried them away into the woods to be murdered.

At Stutthof, priests were among the lowest of the low - in the camp heirachy only Jews ranked below priests. *Juden und Pfaffen* (Jews and Priests) were routinely allocated the worst tasks and the worst punishments. It was for example they who were allocated the cleansing of the camp latrines, a task that involved Jewish inmates

shovelling excrement whilst standing waist deep in the pit and handing full buckets up to priests for emptying.

It is worth noting that many young Polish priests were offered their freedom by the Kommandant on the same basis as that available to Jehovah's Witnesses. All they had to do was sign an Erklarüng claiming German ancestry as well as renouncing their faith. Few succumbed so most literally ended up dying for their faith and their nationality.

Treated as badly or worse than the Polish priests were those of other nationalities. The experiences of one-such, the Lithuanian Stasys Yla, (Prisoner No. 21257) had had to flee his country for Berlin in 1940 to avoid arrest by the Russians as the author of a book exposing the threat posed by the Communist underground movement in his native land. With Operation Barbarossa, the German invasion of Russia, Yla was able to return home but was promptly arrested by the Gestapo and was shipped to Stutthof on the back of an open truck on the 25th March 1943. Once there he and his fellow priests were treated abysmally. They were flogged weekly and subjected to extra attention from the SS at all times. They were also placed on all the most onerous daily work details.

The other religious inmates present at Stutthof were Jehovah's Witnesses. They were grouped together in a single barracks hut but as a group their faith and courage impressed other prisoners and even some SS Guards. An Austrian inmate in the same block was later sent to Auschwitz where he described the so-called Bible Scholars (Bibelforscher) to the author Tibor Wohl: "They needed their bread desperately, since they were famished. But what did they do? They collected all the bread they had, took half of it and gave the other half to their…spiritual brothers, who came in ravenous from other camps. And they welcomed them and kissed them. Before they ate, they prayed, and afterwards their faces beamed with happiness. They said that nobody was hungry anymore. So you see, then I thought to

myself, 'These are true Christians.' That was how I always imagined they should be."

Several of the Jehovah's Witnesses in Stutthof were of German stock and came from a small but thriving pre-war community in Danzig. Hermine Schmidt was one of them. Her family chose to become Witnesses in 1920 and she was raised as Jehovah's Witness from her birth five years later. Then in 1943, aged only seventeen, she was arrested and taken to Gestapo Headquarters in Karrenwall (now ul Okopowa). There she was interrogated for seven days to reveal the names of other Jehovah's Witnesses before facing a swift trial which condemned her to imprisonment in Stutthof. There like all her co-religionists she was required to wear a purple badge designating the nature of her religious offence against the Third Reich.

On account of her age and fitness she was made to perform heavy labour but like other religious offenders of German ancestry she was offered her freedom if she renounced her faith. She refused but managed to survive the camp and at the end of the war was evacuated into the Baltic on a disused river barge by the SS. Her barge drifted into Danish territorial waters and she was rescued on 5th May 1945.

Other German citizens from the Danzig area could be and were imprisoned at Stutthof for short periods of re-education, commonly for two months. The grounds for detention would be officially recorded as *Erziehungshaft* meaning instructional arrest. Their actual offence often involved malingering or unwillingness to work.

Helene Loth (Prisoner No. 20038) was one such Reichsdeutsche prisoner. Arrested in Danzig, she was sent to Stutthof on 1st March 1943. Her medical examination on arrival revealed her to be three months pregnant and she was released just over four weeks later on 1st April.

Other prisoners arrived at Stutthof not because of anything they had done but as hostages for the behaviour of other family members. Thus an absentee conscript might be encouraged to surrender for military service by the detention under threat of worse punishment

of a parent or sibling as was the case with Antoni Kutz from Neustadt, sent with his wife and sixteen-year-old daughter to Stutthof in September 1943 because his son, Bruno Kutz, had deserted from the Wehrmacht.

Naturally enough Stutthof received its share of those involved in both German and Polish resistance movement. One of the barracks huts in the Old Camp was unique its place in the camp structure even after Stutthof was designated a concentration camp; Block V remained under the control of the Gestapo in Danzig and was used to house those suspected of involvement in underground organisations who were kept separated from all other prisoners pending trial and sentence. Gestapo members attended Block V regularly to interrogate prisoners, sometimes under torture.

Sexual orientation also landed some Germans in Stutthof as could affiliation with a cultural organisation other than the Hitler Youth might also bring a young man to Stutthof. The Scout movement in Poland was regarded with particular suspicion and several Boy Scouts and Scout Masters found themselves in Stutthof.

In the two years leading up to September 1939, the Gestapo secured the convictions of some 30,000 German men accused of homosexual offences. Most served terms in ordinary criminal prisons but about 5,000, commonly those found guilty of enticing others into homosexual activity, ended up in Dachau and other German concentration camps for re-education. The energetic pre-war suppression of homosexuality was not though significantly extended into Nazi occupied countries thereafter. The principal concern was always the sexual orientation of ethnic Germans rather than that of inferior, non-Aryan, conquered races and from 1939 the war pushed the priority of the Gestapo and the SS to the Jewish question and suppressing potential armed resistance to the Third Reich leaving less resources available for anything else. In any event most German men of military age were being conscripted and thus becoming subject to Wehrmacht discipline which pushed overt homosexuals into

punishment units deployed to the Eastern front rather than imprisoning them.

It seems unlikely, therefore, that Stutthof ever contained more than a few compulsory wearers of the pink triangle and those who were there, must have found themselves isolated by both the overt nature of their sexual offences and their German nationality amid the melting pot of races who all had cause to hate the country which had imprisoned and victimised them. Subjected to hard labour and malnutrition, without the support of family or racial groupings to support them, and as earmarked targets for SS brutality, criminalised homosexual prisoners faced dramatically reduced survival opportunities and unsurprisingly an estimated death rate of over 60%.

This is not to say that homosexual inmates were scarce at Stutthof but rather that they probably constituted a dispersed and well-concealed minority among the Poles, Jews and prisoners-of-war who made up the bulk of the camp population at different times.

Jews were of course far from being the single amorphous mass that the label imposed on them implied. There were obvious cultural and religious differences between eastern European Jewry and the Greek Sephardim – Jews descended from those expelled from Spain in 1492 who spoke Ladino, a mixture of Spanish and Hebrew – but at least that had belief and faith in common which many others did not. Despite exposure to nineteenth and twentieth century anti-semitism in France, Germany, Poland, Russia and elsewhere, significant numbers of Jews had assimilated, abandoning their religion and identifying themselves first and foremost as citizens of their chosen nation. For them it came as an enormous shock to find themselves classified and labelled by a religion which had come to mean little to them. To expect them to have much in common - apart from genetic ancestry - with all those they were imprisoned with would be unreasonable, at least until the common cause of shared persecution and suffering provided that unifying factor. The hardest hit of all

seem to have been the non-practising Jews of Germany and Austria, many of whom had served the Kaiser in the First World War and who viewed their nationality with much the same superior pride as their Aryan neighbours did even if such attitudes availed them nought after the Nuremberg laws on Racial Purty were enacted in Germany and the Holocaust began

Early on in its history Stutthof inherited some 450 able-bodied Jews from Danzig but did not until 1944 have a particularly significant Jewish population. Only from 1942 when it was formally accepted for concentration camp status was a role for Stutthof in the clearance of Jews from eastern Europe considered.

Nazi policy pre-war had revolved around persecution to encourage emigration from Germany, extermination having been discounted as impractical but the scale of the issue multiplied dramatically with the invasion of Poland and then Russia. Large-scale shootings and the establishment of Jewish ghettos became the accepted approach until dedicated extermination camps were built. These used gas for mass murder and *The Final Solution* was underway.

There was, however, a competing demand for slave labourers and thus instead of killing all Jews who could be rounded up, the requirement came for Auschwitz to separate arrivals into the able-bodied to go on to work camps and those too infirm, too young or too old who would be exterminated as quickly as feasible. Stutthof at the hub of its own web of work sub-camps had a need for more such labourers as well as which it was also well situated to receive and process transports from the east and then send able-bodied Jews on to other camps like Neuengamme and elsewhere. Thus Stutthof experienced major population growth of inmates who were almost all Jewish.

For Jews deemed fit enough to work by the Auschwitz-Birkenau overseers, a transfer out was frequently the start of an itinerant existence with short stops until the next required task took them elsewhere. Thus Alfred Chimowicz, the manager of a machining

factory was one of 500 metal workers extracted from the Łódź ghetto in 1944, sent to Auschwitz-Birkenau for ten days and then shipped by train to Stutthof. They would be there for only a fortnight. The Chimowicz party included his younger brother, Leon and his sister-in-law together with two of their sons, the youngest having been taken away and presumably murdered by an SS guard on arrival at Auschwitz. Within days Leon would be a desperate witness as his wife and sons were marched away with other mothers and children out of the Stutthof women's camp to an unknown fate.

Alfred Chimowicz was ordered to help select workers to travel to a small factory near Poznan to clean, oil and crate machinery for shipment to Dresden. Among the thirty-one others in the group he helped assemble from his fellow exiles from Łódź were his brother and a seventeen year old from Chodecz in North-West Poland called Roman Halter. Halter was already desperate to get away from Stutthof. Starving, he had caught the eye of two Poles who had lured him to their block with the promise of food. There it slowly dawned on Halter that the price tag would be sexual and he managed to escape by feigning the need to use the toilet before climbing into their bunk. As he later put it in his memoirs, "I lived in fear of my life. Had the two Poles looked for me and found me, they would have murdered me. I discovered that they had an important position in their block, and to murder a person was quite common. They would not have been punished for it." Roman Halter would not only survive Stutthof but soon enough the Dresden firestorm too.

The major camp expansion occurred in 1944 when 75,000 prisoners, especially Hungarian and Polish Jews began to arrive en-masse from Riga, Kaunas, Konigsberg, Bialystok and Lublin. A large influx came with the evacuation of Kaiserwald in Latvia. These were primarily Jews from the liquidation of the Riga, Liepaia and Dvinsk ghettos. A great number of Jews were transferred from Auschwitz whilst other inmates came from the Pawiak prison in Warsaw and from the evacuation camp at Pruszkow after the Warsaw uprising of 1944.

In all tens of thousands of people, perhaps more than 100,000, were deported to the Stutthof camp including non-Jewish Poles and Jews from all of Europe.

The plight of the transferees was pitiful as Maria Suszynska witnessed. "They arrived in a horrifying physical state, usually from other camps mainly Auschwitz to die here. They plodded on and on fatigued, with black faces, hair growing from their skin in bristle. They plodded on and on staring with their huge black eyes with what seemed to be an inhuman expression. They wore neither sweaters or jackets only torn summer dresses, through the tears in which their grey bodies could be seen. They were without vests, gaunt with their pointed shoulders, sunken chests – they were more like some weird ugly birds. In their hands they gripped pieces of bread but were unable to eat. Were they aware where they were once more being taken?"

Nor was Stutthof usually the end of the road and onward transfers to other camps and back into Germany were frequent. Thus the first batch of 2,500 Jewish women from Auschwitz was swiftly sent on to work in factories across the Baltic region. Not that Jews who remained at Stutthof were intended to survive once their useful working life was exhausted, usually within months and where survival did occur it was frequently an arbitrary outcome of circumstances and luck as the stories of individual inmates in this book clearly demonstrate. Thus, Abba Noar, a 16 year old Lithuanian Jew deported to Stutthof from the Kaunus Ghetto in 1944 lived to see liberation as did Judit Beker (later to become Judy Meisel) and her older sister Rachel but not their mother, Mina Beker, who was killed in the gas chamber at Stutthof on 21st November 1944, after five months in the camp.

The fourteen year old Judit had been selected to share her mother's fate but was pulled out of the line by an SS guard perhaps because she was young and blonde-haired. Unsure what to do, Judit was shouted at by her mother to run and it was her obedience that saved

her life. It was not to be the only fortuitous element in Judit and Rachel Beker's survival.

Selected in January 1945 as two of a 1,000 prisoner column for an eight mile march to Nickelswade, an *umschlagplatz* (a terminus used for killing and resolving onward transportation to other camps), the Bekers, at the rear, used the distraction provided by allied aircraft to hide first in a ditch and then in a coal hut. A Russian POW working on an SS owned farm discovered them, fed them, got them a bath and change of clothes and sent them on their way, posing as Anna and Uta, two Lithuanian Catholic girls, to a convent across the Vistula.

The nuns nursed Rachel who had typhus but by the time she recovered Judit was very ill and Rachel insisted on taking her to a hospital in Danzig. Somehow Rachel befriended the German wife of an SS officer and the family gave them work in return for food and shelter and took them with them when they fled on a boat to Denmark. Torpedoed and clinging to wreckage, the girls were rescued by a fishing boat where they gained places with their false names in a German refugee centre.

Only on 5th May 1945 when they discovered the war was over did they reveal their true identities to an astonished Red Cross worker. Eventually they both settled in Canada where they were reunited with their brother, Abe, who had survived Dachau.

The speed of the German advance into Russia and the early collapse of Soviet resistance brought a new problem; that of large groups of Soviet Prisoners of War, all of them starving and regarded by their captors as sub-human and good for nothing except slave labour. For them confinement in a *Stalag* and treatment in accordance with the Geneva Convention was never an option contemplated by the German High Command. Instead they were transported to concentration camps and one of the nearest to the Eastern Front was Stutthof which in the course of a few months received several

thousand Russian POWs and later Hungarians once their country ceased to be a German ally.

Aldo Coradello was one of the more unusual prisoners sent to Stutthof in 1943 for expressing ant-fascist views, an unpardonable offence for the Italian Vice-Consul in Danzig. Important enough to be spared the worst rigours of concentration camp life, he used his time to gather and memorise the evidence which he was eventually able to share with the world at the post-war trials of Stutthof personnel. In particular he was able to recall in detail the day that around fifty Russian prisoners-of-war arrived, all of them lacking one or more limbs or their sight, dressed in filthy rags and in deep despair. Their plight made a deep impression on Coradello especially after he heard Oberscharführer Arno Chemnitz describe them as 'Russian rubbish.' Sadly all he could do for them was stand witness to their fate.

Promised that they were being taken to a convalescent home, the crippled soldiers were led away to be murdered that same day. In all probability each received only a bullet to the back of the neck.

Scandanavia too was unusually well-represented in Stutthof.

Norway contained more than its fair share of Fascists supportive of both the German invasion of 9th April 1940 and the short-lived collaborationist government of Vidkun Quisling. Whilst the general population were sharply divided between acceptance and civil disobedience (or even armed resistance) the police service contained a proportion of pro-Nazi officers. This was significant given the role given to the civilian police in 1942 of rounding up Norwegian Jews.

After the sham trial and execution of Gunnar Eilifsen, the Oslo Police Chief who had refused to arrest young women for failing to report to the authorities for near-certain transportation as slave labourers, it was decided that all police officers should swear allegiance to the Third reich and join the Nasjonal Samling, the only political party authorised to exist in Norway by the Nazis.

A total of 271 officers who failed to join the party were arrested in the so-called *Aktion Polarkreis* and after periods of imprisonment and forced labour elsewhere were gathered together and shipped en masse on an arduous journey be sea and on by rail car and then open narrow-gauge train trucks to Stutthof where they were subjected to constant pressure to join the Nazis and be returned home. In an unprecedented display of unity they all continued to refuse to bend and remained in the separate Germanenlager compound just outside the main camp until the 258 survivors were liberated by the advancing Russian army.

Among the Norwegians was Reidar Kvammen an international Norwegian footballer with 51 caps for Norway to his name and 17 goals. He was a prominent member of the Norwegian bronze-medal winning team that knocked Germany out of the 1936 Olympics and played in the World Cup two years later. At club level, he scored 202 goals for Viking. Like other compatriots arrested for refusing to join the Nazis he was arrested and imprisoned first in Stavanger and then was then held in Grini concentration camp until December 1943 when he was sent to Stutthof. He survived the camp and lived until 1998.

A fellow officer who was less fortunate was Jahn Iver Kornbrekke a policeman from Årdal but actually born to Norwegian parents in America returning to Norway only following his father's death in an industrial accident. Kornbrekke died of stomach ulceration on 14th May 1944, in Stutthof's camp hospital. He was, however, one of only thirteen fatalities among the Norwegian policemen. In the main though the Norwegian policeman were fit and healthy and their resourcefulness became legendary as was their willingness to engage in acts of sabotage and disruption.

Among the Norwegians were civilians like Gunnar Jørgensen who was studying mechanical engineering including jet propulsion at the Hanover Technique Hochschule. Jørgensen When Germany invaded Norway Gunnar he sought to return to Norway, believing his studies

would contribute to the German war effort but was precluded from doing so by the intervention of the Gestapo. He was only finally allowed to return home to take up a police post in Kristiansund. He then attempted to escape to England to join the resistance only for his small fishing boat to be caught in a storm. Arrested and initially imprisoned at Flastad prison, Gunnar was transferred on 8th December, 1943 to Stutthof from where he was liberated on 5th May, 1945, returning home to marry his fiance, Solveig Sundling and eventually to emigrate to Canada.

The fact that so few of the Norwegians died despite harsh conditions, poor food rations, every day violence and disease, degradation and hate, torture and blows has to be due to their strong communal support for each other as well as the food parcels - dried fish and chocolate being particularly prized – that they were sporadically allowed to receive from the Red Cross and their families back in Norway, although these were subject to substantial looting and confiscations in transit by their SS guards. They survived largely on potatoes mixed with anything else available into a type of soup but they were permitted to wear their own police uniforms, were exempt from physical labour, had access to newspapers and pen and paper and several of them kept diaries and wrote memoirs which Tore Jørgensen, the son of, Gunnar Jørgensen, has translated for posterity.

As well as invading Norway on 9th April 1940 Germany also invaded Denmark with the Danish government surrendering within a mere two hours. On 22nd June 1941, the eve of Operation Barbarossa, the invasion of Russia, the Germans demanded the Danish police arrest 339 named members of the Communist Party of Denmark (the DKP), among them a member of parliament called Martin Nielsen. On the 20th August, Nielsen and one hundred and six of the arrestees in Copenhagen were transferred from Vestre Prison to the Horserød Camp and in December 1942, Nielsen was handed over to the Gestapo for interrogation.

In August 1943, the German dissolved the Danish government, and took direct control of the camp where Nielsen was being held. Two months later, on 2nd October 1943, Nielsen was one of a group of 143 men and 7 women, all communists, transferred to Stutthof. The deportees travelled on the S/S Wartheland to Swinemünde and then by cattle truck to the camp which was to house them for the next fifteen months. Twenty-two of Nielsen's Communist colleagues died but despite his age, 43 at the time of his deportation, Nielsen survived the imprisonment and the death march of January 1945 finally returning home to Copenhagen in June 1945 - not however before the liberating Red Army had on 10th March insisted on despatching him on foot to Moscow.

Ragnhild Nikoline Andersen was another Danish Communist activist and trade unionist sent to Stutthof with her close friend Inger Gamburg. Andersen and Gamburg together with four of the five other women imprisoned with them survived in the camp from October 1943 returning home to continue their political careers. Andersen also wrote her account of Stutthof under the title *Vi blev reddet denne gang* (We Were Saved That Time).

Unlike the Norwegian policemen who were tough enough and well-organised against the predations of other prisoners, the Danish communists were potentially much more vulnerable. Identified by their German captors as fellow Aryans, Scandanavian prisoners could send mail and receive letters and packages from home as well as Swedish and Danish Red Cross packages containing cheese, wurst, butter, dried milk, fat, oats, crackers, canned pork, sardines in tomato sauce, sugar, sweets, cigarettes and tobacco. Wieslaw Kielar recounts how Russian and Hungarian prisoners would beat Danish prisoners half to death in order to get hold of whatever remnants of their Red Cross packages the SS guards had allowed to be delivered which the Danes tended to conceal on their persons rather than leaving them unguarded in their huts.

That said some of the Scandinavian prisoners were segregated from the rest of Stutthof's population by barbed wire fences, but were altruistic enough to pass life-saving scraps to the most needy young people in the camp. Roman Halter described one such experience: 'I came upon a block within the camp that was fenced off from all the other blocks. As I drew closer I heard a man inside say in German, 'Here you are, boy, take that,' and he threw a small paper bag out of the window and over the wire fence.' The paper bag contained a number of bread crusts; the donor was a Danish resistance fighter contact with whom, if discovered by the kapos, was likely to be punishable by death. Not for the Dane but for the Jew.

The Scandanavian contingent in Stutthof were joined in 1944 by a number of Finnish seamen. The Russians had fought a brief Winter War with Finland from November 1939 to March 1940 with the Finns ceding territory to the invaders. The German invasion of Russia in 1941 was seized upon by the Finns as a means of recovering lost ground and prestige and they duly declared war on Russia, allowing the Germans to cross the Finnish borders to attack Leningrad. The Continuation War lasted until a ceasefire was declared on 5th September 1944. Until then Finnish merchant vessels were carrying supplies to and from German ports but with the ceasefire, any ships in ports were seized by the Germans.

Four Finnish vessels were stranded in Danzig, the S/S Bore VI, the S/S Mercator, the S/S Wappu and the S/S Ellen and their crews were given the option of imprisonment for the duration of the war or of joining the German marines. They opted for the former. In total the crews comprised seventy-eight men and twelve women – cooks, kitchen hands and cleaners. The men included several youngsters who'd been unable to sign up for the Finnish military, and their ship's captain, Vihtori Jansen.

The new Finnish prisoners with leaders, who included a man named Ingmar Fredriksson from Helsingfors, were sent to Stutthof in two batches, arriving a week apart, late in October. The men were housed

in four newer barrack huts comprising Block III some two kilometres north of the main gate while the women were placed in Blocks I and VIII of the Old Camp or according to the record kept by Gunnar Jorgensen in the sewing room in the infirmary. Most of them spoke only Finnish and were therefore somewhat isolated within Stutthof. Although a prisoner called Stefanson from Bergen spoke Finnish and was able to translate for them on occasion apart from him there was limited ability to communicate with the other Scandinavians imprisoned there.

Ten of the Finns were released after a short time but the rest were detained until 1945. Among them was the sixteen-year-old Aarne Kovvala whose experiences of Stutthof are outlined later.

A small number of British POWs also found themselves in Stutthof for no readily discernible reason. Indeed a couple of them were among prisoners allocated to help Rudolph Spanner at Danzig's Anatomical Research Institute and it was they who are one possible source of false information that the Germans were routinely manufacturing soap from human bodies in industrial quantities.

One of the most notorious SS units from an allied perspective, even if the numbers enrolled at any given time never exceeded thirty men, was the British Free Corps formally established in January 1944 and comprising volunteers drawn from captured troops held in prisoner-of-war camps. They were equipped from April 1944 in uniforms bearing a Union Flag on the arm and three heraldic leopards as a collar patch.

Two enrolled members of the Corps ended up as inmates of Stutthof. Thomas Freeman (Private 5831031) of No.7 Commando was being held at Stalag XVIIIa at the time he was recruited (as Sergeant Tony Mitchell) into the British Free Corps alongside a friend, a Belgian national called Theo Menz, who was using false papers bearing the alias of a South African Sergeant, Theo Ellsmore. Freeman saw recruitment into the Corps as an opportunity to escape and until that was possible planned to sabotage the Corps from the inside. He had

the sense to seek permission from his Regimental Sergeant-Major for his plans, a move which ensured that a post-war court martial for treason resulted in his acquittal on all charges.

Freeman's successful endeavours resulted in new factionalisation within the Corps and fifteen former prisoners-of-war seeking to return to imprisonment rather than continuing to serve in the unit. Freeman and Menz were however identified as ringleaders in this mass defection, charged with mutiny and transhipped to Stutthof. There Menz was reportedly murdered but Freeman escaped in November 1944, although it is more likely he was in a satellite camp rather than the main concentration camp when he did so. Whichever was the case, Freeman reached the advancing Soviets and was ultimately repatriated to Britain in March 1945.

Lithuania, like most of the Baltic states, had a long and complex history in relation to Russia and to the Austro-Hungarian Empire and thus in the twentieth century with Germany. As a country whose existence was constantly threatened by the Soviet Union, many Lithuanians looked to Germany as a potential saviour. The example of priests who were encouraged to take refuge in Berlin only to become victims of the Nazi regime is explored below but it is less easy to sympathise with other Lithuanian collaborators who were ultimately arrested by the Germans and imprisoned in Stutthof. One of them was an army captain and prominent member of the Lithuanian Activist Front named Jonas Noreika.

Noreika was born in 1910 in Šukioniai. Strongly anti-Semitic and the author of pro-Hitler literature, he led a group of partisans armed by the Germans in the general uprising against the Russian invaders which began on the 22nd June 1941 and the following month he gave the orders for the Plungė Massacre in which 1,800 Jews were taken hostage in their synagogue and murdered in batches over the course of several days. By August he held an official position as a district governor (responsible among other things for establishing new Jewish ghettos and confiscation of Jewish property) a position from

which he was dismissed on 23rd February 1943 for his failure to carry out an order to establish a new Waffen-SS division for service in the Wehrmacht.

On 17th March 1943, 46 Lithuanian politicians, intellectuals and religious figures were arrested by the Nazis and shipped to Stutthof on the 26th and 27th. Noreika was one of them. The new Lithuanian inmates led a privileged existence in Stutthof. Exempt from labour, permitted to wear civilian clothes, allowed to study and write letters they were also allowed to receive regular parcels from home including foodstuffs. Unsurprisingly, Noreika survived Stutthof. He was evacuated in 1944 and eventually liberated by the Red Army. He did not however live very long after that. Arrested for further anti-Soviet activity he was executed on 26th February 1947. Despite his active role in the Holocaust he remains a national hero to some Lithuanians.

By way of contrast the treatment and fate of Lithuanian Catholic priests in Stutthof could not have been more different as has already been shown even when, like Stasys Yla, they were transported to Stutthof among other prominent prisoners, in his case as part of a group of a group of twenty-nine Lithuanians, comprising army officers, teachers, public officials, students and the director of a glassworks company, Colonel Māciokis, shipped to the camp on 25th March 1943. Yla as a priest was swiftly separated from his friends and countrymen on arrival.

The second Kommandant of Stutthof, Paul Werner Hoppe, hardly ever bothered to greet new arrivals at the camp and yet for reasons never explained he made an exception for these Lithuanian arrivals inspecting them in person, accompanied by his assistant, Oberscharführer Arno Chemnitz. Perhaps it was simply because Yla and his companions were the first new intake of political prisoners Hoppe had seen.

Another Lithuanian imprisoned at Stutthof from 1943 was a man who was dangerously both a priest and an intellectual, the economist,

Professor Vladas Jurgutis. Jurgutis survived the war returning home at 60 year old but he never returned to public life.

Then there was the printer Vladislovas Telksnys who was part of a group of sixteen intellectuals calling themselves *The Press Group*. They were arrested by the Gestapo on 27th April 1943 but no attempt was made to interrogate them. Instead they went on trial straight away and two days later were in Stutthof where Telksnys…*went through hell* for nearly a year until fellow Lithuanians were able to collect enough gold to pay the Gestapo to secure his freedom. He was 29-years-old and at the time of his release weighed only 38 kilograms.

The writer, Balys Sruoga, was another Lithuanian inmate, a famed poet he described his experiences in Stutthof in *The Forest of Gods*, a novel that has become part of the Lithuanian literary canon.

In 1944 around a hundred French SS Legionnaires were sent to Stutthof, probably for refusal to obey orders, as were a group of mutineer German seamen. Sentenced to hard labour and flogging, few survived more than a few weeks in the camp.

The plot of 20th July 1944 to assassinate Hitler led to a massive round-up of potential conspirators and their families, as well as not a few denounced without evidence by enemies seeking to settle old scores. A number of them ended up imprisoned in Stutthof including members of Claus von Stauffenberg's family and 150 German officers labelled *Haudegen* suspected of collaboration with the allies to secure an end to the war. Their privileged treatment in Stutthof was in sharp contrast to that of run of the mill prisoners. Separated in their own barracks, they wore their own clothes, were not required to use their camp numbers, could walk freely around the camp up to the 21.00 curfew, could borrow books from the SS library and were exempt from any labour apart from chopping food for their stoves, cooking and cleaning for themselves. In time they were allocated two Russian prisoners-of-war to serve as their maids. Both Claus von Stauffenberg's mother-in-law, Baroness von Lerchenfeld, and Mika Stauffenberg spoke fluent Russian and were thus able to garner a deal

of information about how the lowliest of prisoners in Stutthof were treated.

The orders governing the treatment of these German aristocrats and officers came from Himmler himself who viewed them as potential hostages in an uncertain future but not even Himmler could protect them from typhus, dysentery and the other diseases endemic in the camp. Anna von Lerchenfeld herself would die of pneumonia after being transferred to Matzkau, a short-lived transit camp nearer Danzig.

From 1944 of course a significant number of the Jews transported to Stutthof were also Lithuanian.

Stutthof from its inception operated as a male camp and it was some ten months before any women were sent there. Then in June 1940 the first trickle of female inmates arrived and numbers grew slowly until the flood of Jewish arrivals from August 1944.

Eminent women imprisoned at Stutthof included Dora Rabinowitz who as Dora Love went on to produce a remarkable book of poems about Stutthof and Eugenia Durys (1921-1994) arrested in 1943 by the Gestapo as an underground activist who used her position with the Gdynia Port Administration to smuggle refugees and couriers onto ships bound for neutral Sweden.

Another was Julia Rodzínska, (born Stanislawa Rodkinska (Prisoner No. 40992) who arrived in Stutthof in 1944. Her experience and fate were not untypical for Poles in the camp. A teacher and Dominican sister, she had been held since 12th July 1943 in the Łukiškés Prison in Vilnius. She had been arrested by the Gestapo for no greater crime than teaching Polish and providing humanitarian support in the community around her. In a four day cattle wagon journey she was transported as a political prisoner to Stutthof where she coped with the harsh labour regime and poor diet at Stutthof for only a few months, dying on 20th February 1945 of typhus. She was 45 years old.

In 1942 following the liquidation of the Warsaw Ghetto, a five-year old girl was transported to Stutthof with her mother, a Polish Jew. They were among 11,000 Jews sent to labour camps unlike the majority who had gone to Treblinka or been shot out of hand. The little girl's name was Ingoushka Petrov, her father was of mixed Russian and German descent and she had been born in Warsaw in 1937.

Ingoushka's story is unusual. There were children in Stutthof but they were few in number and the odds for their survival were not high. Somehow Ingoushka's mother, Mascha Petrov, kept her daughter by her side and ensured she was fed and safe, a near impossible feat for a Jewess in Stutthof. Her good fortune arose from the circumstances of their incarceration and from the humanitarian intervention of a kapo, Peter Steiner.

Marscha and Ingoushka Petrov arrived at Stutthof in 1943 as hostages for the collaboration of Ingoushka's father, an aeronautical scientist, in the V2 rocket programme at Peenemünde. As such they were housed in the Gestapo-controlled Block V. Marscha was allocated work in the camp laundry while Ingoushka was required to attend lessons with Fraulein Gloge, a kindly hunchbacked woman, in the *kinderschuppen*, a small hut in which selected children who might prove suitable candidates for adoption by childless Aryan couples were gathered. Ingoushka was permitted to return each evening to sleep with her mother and Mascha Petrov's Lithuanian friend from the laundry, Annie Jadkowska.

The friend came to a sad end. Accused of passing notes to Russian prisoners-of-war, Annie Jadkowska was publically hanged and her blockmates, including the young Ingoushka, were required to attend. As a secondary consequence of her friendship with a deemed spy or saboteur, Marscha lost her job in the laundry and was placed on a kommando unloading and breaking rocks, tasks which would have swiftly killed her had Peter Steiner, her kapo, not managed to engineer her transfer into the kitchens.

Steiner went on to save them again as the camp evacuations began in 1945. Prewarned of the SS plan to liquidate the *kinderschuppen*, killing the few remaining children, he secreted the eight-year-old away, hiding Ingoushka in her mother's bunk. A few hours later the Petrovs tagged onto one of the forced marches out of the camp towards Danzig, took refuge in a ditch and played dead as allied aircraft strafed the straggling column, and found a home with partisans in the forest for the last few weeks of the war, a survival story improbable enough to be the invention of an imaginative novelist.

Many years later writing about her time in Stutthof, Ingoushka's recollections, although a child's, were clear and explicit. *'I got used to the stench, the shouting and the snarling dogs which never barked,'* she said. By then she had been briefly reunited with her father before his death and had successfully reinvented herself as the film star, Ingrid Pitt.

Children were in fact unlikely to arrive in Stutthof at all. The most common fate was separation from their parents as their ghettos were liquidated and death by shooting after short journeys away from the towns they came from.

Two exceptions were Chaja Verblunsky (Stutthof Inmate 43971) and Riva Rubin (Rifka Rubinovic) who were both fortunate enough to be able to pass as older than their true ages - about twelve and thirteen respectively. Their documentation at Stutthof falsely gives Chaja's year of birth as 1931 and Riva's as 1932 and it was a stratagem that saved them from immediate selection on arrival for gassing.

Both Chaja and Riva were Lithuanian Jews and each came from the Kovno Ghetto (Kaunus) by railway cattle car arriving at Stutthof with their mothers on 13th July 1944. Each had also seen a younger brother removed for execution in the Kovno Kinderaktion of 27th-28th March 1944. Chaja's younger brother, Avram, was only five years old and she also lost her father, a tailor who was sent to Dachau and did not survive the war.

Chaja and Riva did not knew each other in Kovno only meeting after they arrived at Stutthof but they became bosom friends in the camp

and later together at the Elbing sub-camp where they were put to work digging trenches.

The *Ziguener* - the German umbrella term for the gypsies - covered both the Sinti of Germany and Western Europe, and the Roma of Austria and Eastern Europe. Both groupings were designated by the Nazis as racially inferior and as enemies of the Reich to be annihilated. From 1939 compulsory registration applied to them and the process of transporting them out of Germany was underway. In fact most ended up housed alongside the Jews in their designated ghettos. Over 5,000 gypsies were shipped to the Łódź Ghetto for example.

On 16th January 1942 Himmler issued an order for the removal of all Roma and Sinti to concentration camps, an order supplemented on 29th January 1943 by regulations specifying a new Zigeunerlager at Auschwitz-Birkenau as the mandated destination.

Some 23,000 gypsies were transported that year, all wearing a black triangle stitched onto the civilian clothing they were permitted to retain. They were also housed in family groupings, a dispensation which merely ensured that entire families were gassed together.

By 1944 only 2,000 gypsies were still alive in Auschwitz although a handful of military veterans of the Great War had been released alongside a small number of gypsies in mixed marriages who had Aryan family members outside the camp to advocate for them. In the middle of the year 1408 gypsies were shipped out to Buchenwald as slave labourers and the rest were dispersed to other camps. Some certainly reached Stutthof given Jewish survivor testimonies which refer to interactions with Roma and Sinti inmates but no apparent details or numbers appear to be available.

The largest ever uprising in Nazi-occupied Europe commenced in Warsaw at 1700 hours on 1st August 1944. The uprising which led to several weeks of vicious street fighting had been planned by Polish resistance groups to capitalise on the approaching Soviet forces pushing towards the eastern perimeter of the city. Frustratingly the

Red Army failed to support the Poles. The Russian advance stalled for no obvious reason allowing 17,000 German troops to focus all their efforts on subduing the uprising which was done with extreme brutality. Over 16,000 partisans were killed and mass executions removed between 150,000 and 200,000 of the approximately one million Polish civilians still living in Warsaw.

As early as 5th August the Germans were carrying out house to house clearances and demolishing whole areas of the city, beginning a process that would effectively wipe Warsaw off the map while the Red Army stood by and let it happen.

The clearances flushed out hidden Jews who had survived the liquidation of the Warsaw Ghetto in 1943 but the German goal was to deport every one of the surviving Polish civilians. Many were sent first to the Prosków Transit Camp and then on to Stutthof. There they were processed and many were allocated Stutthof prisoner numbers although the camp could not cope with such a massive influx of new prisoners and so within days or, at the latest, weeks most new inmates were transferred elsewhere as slave labourers. Many found themselves at Neuengamme near Hamburg or its satellite camps. For female prisoners that often meant Hannover-Langenhagen with its incessant need for armaments workers.

The records of the Arolsen Archives demonstrate the commonality of transfer dates and destinations for former Warsaw residents displaced as a consequence of the uprising. Civilians deported to Stutthof on 31st August 1944 and swiftly moved on included Alexandra Nowak (a seamstress eventually liberated at Bergen-Belsen), Stanisław Wolborski (a woodworker who survived the war and married another slave labourer, Helena Gwardnak on 17th July 1945), Krystyna Zawierucha (Prisoner no. 87225, a corset-maker who died post-liberation in hospital near Bergen-Belsen), Maria Szumidło (a nineteen year old student eventually liberated from Bergen-Belsen), and Józef Hryncewicz (who eventually died as a slave labourer in the Blohm & Voss submarine yards at the Hamburg-Steinwerder sub-

camp of Neuengamme). In total over 6,000 Stutthof deportees were sent on to Neuengamme and its sub-camps.

Surviving camp records show that in addition to the major groups of inmates outlined above, Stutthof housed small numbers of prisoners from an extraordinary list of other countries including America, Austria, Belgium, France, Greece, Italy, the Netherlands, Romania, Slovakia, Spain, Sweden, Switzerland, Turkey and Yugoslavia

Irrespective of nationality, race, creed, sexuality or criminality many Stutthof inmates would become *Muselmenn*, not a categorisation as such but rather a term describing those prematurely aged inmates so worn-down by hard labour and malnutrition that they presented as mere ghosts of the people they once were and who had lost the will to live. Essentially they were Stutthof's badly-starved, walking dead, waiting to be carried off by disease or to be selected for extermination by their SS guards.

Antoni Kasztelan *Franciszek Rogaczewski* *Gunner Eilifsen*

Gunnar Jorgensen *Wladsimierz Steyer* *Ingrid Pitt*

Martin Nielsen, and Reidar Kvammen

Erika Mannheimer, Zigi Shipper & Manfred Goldberg, and Balys Sruoga

Jahn Iver Kornbrekke, and Aarne Kovvala

Marian Kampinski, Stasys Yla, and Vladislovas Telksnys

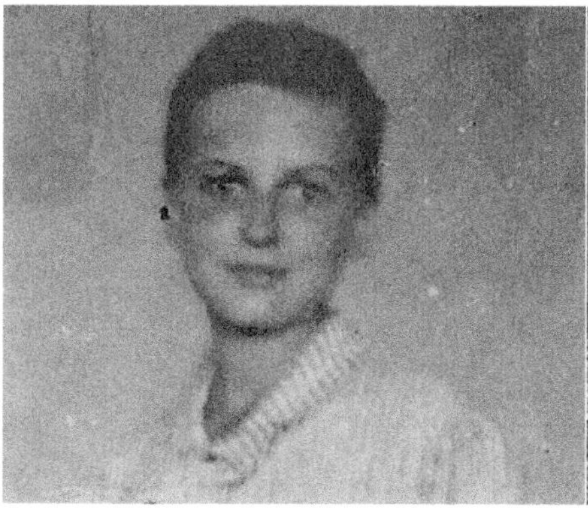
Dora Roth

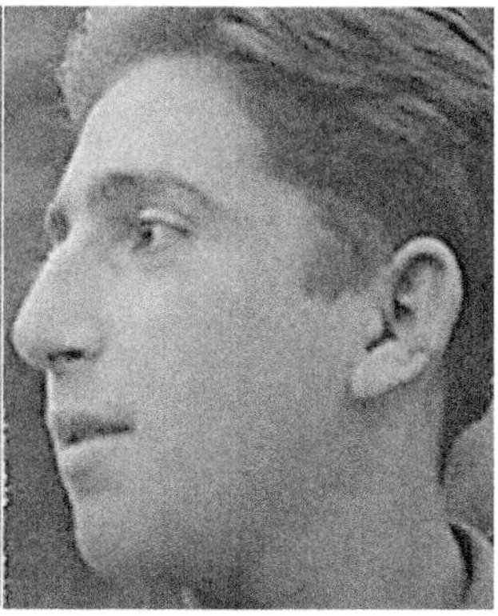
Abba Noar

Chaja Verblunsky

Mina Beker

Judy & Rachel Beker

Jan Rostafiński

Helena Katz

Franciszek Sokół

Esther Lurie (self portrait)

Father Henryk Malak

Sister Julia Rodzinska

Alfons Olszewski (2nd from left in his Polish sailing team)

Ragnhild Nikoline Andersen

Yehuda and Dita Zupovich

Rudolf Ostrihansky

Wacław Jurek

Ryszard Szymanik

Vladis Jurgitis

Therese, Max and Marga & Alfred Steinhardt

Inmate uniform Stutthof

PART 5
THE SS

DURING THE PERIOD from 1939 when Stutthof was directly controlled by the Danzig Police Praesidium and thus by Albert Forster, its SS personnel grew in number to about two hundred men. About fifty carried out administrative tasks in the Kommandantur, the rest performing guard duties and supervising work details under the command at various times of four officers who became well known to the inmates; SS-Untersturmführer Kurt Mathesius, SS-Obersturmführer Erich Gust, SS-Obersturmführer Alfred Dittman, and SS-Untersturmführer Paul Ehle.

The intended expansion of Stutthof as a designated Concentration Camp was preceded by an increase in SS numbers to 600 men by December 1942 but another significant change occurred following the transfer of decision-making to Theodor Eike and the Concentration Camp Inspectorate he headed in Oranienburg. By the year end all Stutthof's officers from the Kommandant, SS-Sturmbannführer Max Pauly, downwards had been transferred elsewhere and a refreshed structure was in place under SS-Sturmbannführer Paul Werner Hoppe. Many of the NCOs were also replaced and at the same time a third functional team were added to manage all the SS commercial enterprises and to ensure an overall profit was derived from the deployment of all the available slave labour.

By 1944 the total SS personnel at Stutthof exceeded 1000 and by the end of the war over 2000 had served at the camp of whom the names of about 1200 have been identified from the available records. They included several Norwegian SS volunteers as well as 295 female German Aufseherinnen deployed in 1942 when the first significant batches of female prisoners arrived at the camp. In addition after 1943, the SS were reinforced by Ukrainian auxiliaries under SS-Gruppenführer Fritz Katzmann.

A shortage of female guards became an issue after the women's camp at Bromberg in the city of Bydgoscz was set up so in June 1944 the

SS began conscripting women from Danzig and surrounding cities in June 1944, to train as camp guards for Stutthof.

Several major changes occurred at Stutthof during 1944 including wholesale camp expansion, the arrivals of large numbers of Jewish transportees, the use of gas to exterminate Jews deemed useless in terms of their ability to labour for the camp all of which demanded increases in staffing including the recruitment of more female guards.

Between 1939 and 1945 Stutthof had only two Kommandants, Max Pauly until August 1942 when he was appointed to run Neuegamme Concentration Camp near Hamburg, and Pauly's replacement Paul-Werner Hoppe.

Max Pauly (1907-1946) held the rank of SS Standartenführer and was the man charged by the authorities in Danzig with finding a suitable Concentration Camp site and setting it up in September 1939 (see Part I). Pauly was tried by the British in Hamburg for crimes committed at Neuegamme but none of the charges against him related to the operation of the Stutthof Concentration Camp. The guilty verdict resulted in execution by hanging at Hamelin Prison on 8th October 1946.

Paul-Werner Hoppe (1910-1974) who arrived at Stuutthof in September 1942 was an enthusiastic gardener which presumably explains the decorative flower baskets he had placed at the entrance to Stutthof. He held the rank of SS Obersturmbannführer having joined the SS in 1933. In 1936 he married Charlotte Baranowski, herself the daughter of another concentration camp Kommandant.

Hoppe served with the concentration camps inspectorate (the Inspektion der Konzentrationslager) under SS-Obergruppenführer Theodor Eike and helped Eike form the Waffen SS Totenkopf Division in the autumn of 1939. From April 1941, Hoppe commanded an infantry company and early in spring of 1942, was severely wounded in the leg near Novgorod on the Eastern Front. Recovering, he served as head of a guard unit at Auschwitz from July 1942 until he was promoted to become Kommandant of Stutthof.

He ended his SS career as Kommandant of Wöbbelin. a camp. established to house concentration camp prisoners evacuated from other camps to prevent their liberation by the Allies. Wöbbelin was only in existence from 12th February 1945 to 2nd May 1945 when it was liberated by the Americans army but Hoppe evaded immediate capture and was only picked up by the British in April 1946 in Holstein. He spent nearly six months from August 1947 in a prison camp at Watten in Scotland and then in January 1948 was transferred to the internment camp in Fallingbostel. Whilst awaiting extradition to Poland where he would almost certainly have been exected after trial, he managed to escape to Switzerland where he worked as a landscape gardener under a false identity for three years before returning incognito to West Germany. He was arrested on 17th April 1953 in Witten, and tried as an accessory to murder in 1955, receiving a five-year prison sentence. On 4th June 1957 the district court in Bochum extended Hoppe's sentenced to nine years. Given that the majority of deaths at Stutthof occurred under his command, his sentence was surprisingly lenient but by the time he finally faced trial the thirst for judicial vengeance had cooled somewhat. He was released in 1960.

As at January 1945 before the death marches stripped the camps of inmates and Nazi personnel, the SS staff and guards at Stutthof numbered 1,056 and the command structure included at least two men who might be justifiably labelled as psychopaths.

Untersturmführer Kurt Mathesius was dubbed The Butcher of Stutthof by inmates. The former tavern manager was short in stature, thickset and a walking paradox. He appears to have taken great pride in his uniform, his cap badge and high black boots always immaculately shined masking a degenerating physique and the bloated features of an alcoholic. He seems to have had a particular hatred of priests and regularly oversaw sessions of beatings for all the Lithuanian pfaffan. As described by Stasys Yla, Mathesius would have each priest in turn stretched over a sawhorse, their arms and feet held firmly by guards as ten hefty lashes were administered. Unable to

leave the task to his subordinates, Mathesius would take the whip himself until his strength ran out before handing it back for others to finish off the task.

The other notably brutal SS figure at Stutthof was Hauptsturmführer Theodore Traugott Meyer (1902-1948) formerly an electrician before he joined the NSDAP and SS in 1931. From April 1938-December 1940 Meyer was an engineer at Dachau concentration camp and from January 1941 the protective custody camp leader at Ravensbrück. A year later, in January 1942, he transferred to join Paul Werner Hoppe at Stutthof helping organise the evacuation of in January 1945 and then following Hoppe to Wöbbelin. After the liberation of Wöbbelin by the U.S. Army, Meyer was arrested, sent to Poland for trial and executed by hanging. A self-servingly plaintive confession penned in prison, blaming others for ordering the offences he had committed, did nothing to save him from the gallows.

Other infamously sadistic SS guards included Oberscharführer Ewold Foth, originally a farmer and a practising Lutheran, and Oberscharführer Arno Chemnitz, in civilian life a hotel porter and an early Nazi Party recruit – his party card is dated 1923 – and whose favoured weapons were a plaited wire whip and a rubber bludgeon.

A list of known SS guards at Stutthof is set out as Appendix I at the back of this book. The average age of the 1270 SS guards deployed in September 1939 was 24 years old, the youngest being 17 and the oldest 52. Although all were of German extraction, 344 were from Danzig while others were from the Baltic coast rather than from Germany and some were, surprisingly, Mennonites.

Mennonites are an Anabaptist religious group with common ethnic origins named after a Freislander called Menno Simons (1496-1561) who first codified the teachings of the original Swiss founders. By 1939 significant Mennonite communities lived along the Baltic coast around Danzig with over fifty Mennonite families living in the village of Stutthof and farming in the area. Despite their religion, Mennonites had been early and vocal supporters of Hitler and some

local Mennonites served as SS guards at Stutthof. Indeed the existence of a well-established Mennonite presence in the vicinity of the camp was itself an attraction drawing other German Mennonites to volunteer to serve there. Two such were SS-Unterscharführer Kurt Janzen, and SS Scharführer Heinz Löwen. The latter received a sentence of five years imprisonment after the war.

It is also probable that another SS guard named Schröder was of Mennonite origin. Schröder was charged with participating in the shooting of those women from a contingent of 1,000 Jewesses who became too exhausted to work on ditching and sugar beet harvesting but the charges were dismissed for lack of evidence.

Not all the guards were either SS or of German extraction hence the deployment of the Trawnicki. Named after their assembly and training facility near Lublin, the first Trawnikimanner (or Wachmänner) were recruited by SS-Gruppenführer Odilo Globocnik between September 1941 and March 1942. They were captured Red Army soldiers (mostly Ukrainians and Russians) who volunteered to serve as SS auxiliaries. The supposedly voluntary nature of their service is questionable since in the Prison-of-War camps in which they had been held starvation, disease and freezing cold conditions were prevalent and enlistment by the SS could literally be seen as a choice of life over death. Compared to remaining and dying in a Stalag, paid service in Polish Zlotys with free rations and medical care was no real choice at all.

Clad in a variety of black, khaki and grey uniforms (the only common elements being a black forage cap bearing the totenkopf emblem - the skull and crossbones - and black boots), their primary duties, following six weeks to six months of training (the period depended on assessments of ability and the extent to which they could understand and use the German language) involved rounding up and murdering Jews and partisans both at large in the German occupied territories and at Auschwitz-Birkenau, Treblinka, Majdenek and Sobibor.

Trawniki recruitment was broadened to include volunteers in occupied Eastern Europe whose families might otherwise face deportation to Germany as forced labourers as well as forced conscripts and by May 1943 their rates of pay were comparable with similar ranks in the Wehrmacht and the SS itself.

By March 1943, some 700 Trawniki could be spared for concentration camp duties where they commonly took over the most distasteful tasks such as overseeing the gassing of Jewish inmates. They were not particularly trusted, not least because drunkenness and disciplinary issues were rife among them, and they were seldom allocated to sentry and guard duties except as part of mixed groups containing regular SS men.

The precise number of Trawniki under SS-Gruppenführer Fritz Katzmann. allocated to Stutthof in 1943 is unknown but it cannot have been more than a handful because the majority went to Sachsenhausen (about 550) or Flossenbürg (about 130) with several other camps also receiving a small detachment. Those known to have served at Sutthof included Unterscharführer Alexander Kruklis and Arkady Andreyev, rank unknown.

The first female concentration camp guards, *Aufseherinnen,* trained at Ravensbrück, were deployed to Auschwitz and Majdenek in 1942. None were at that time required at Stutthof despite the camp having a small contingent of female inmates because it was still officially a male camp. That was soon to change.

The term *Aufseherin* referred to a female overseer and the recruits aged 17 to 45 years old were generally from a lower or middle class background and without relevant work experience. Many of them had been cooks or domestic workers, or hairdressers or held similar occupations.

German newspaper advertisements sought female volunteers to show their love for the Reich by joining the *Weibliche SS-Gefolge* (female SS followers) which together with the League of German Girls channelled many potential volunteers towards the recruiting

authorities. Despite the nature of the duties, becoming one of the *Aufseherinnen* could be a relatively attractive option for lower class women since it attracted higher pay than domestic service or factory labour, allowed recruits to wear impressive uniforms and carry officially sanctioned weapons such as whips, although not pistols, and gave them power of life and death over other human lives. Even so, recruitment of volunteers could not match growing demand and conscription was soon put in place.

By 1944 with the Germans losing the war and manpower for the war effort a growing problem the German Labour Exchange (the *Reichsarbeitsdienst*) was charged with conscripting women away from work in factories and other occupations to serve as concentration camp guards. Commonly trained at Ravensbrück, forty-seven such female recruits were then allocated to Stutthof and another one hundred and fifty to Stuthhof's network of satellite camps.

Females recruits could not however serve in the SS. As guards they were always auxiliaries and employees of the Reich (*Reichsangestellte*) and so weren't given ranks equivalent to male SS personnel. Instead the supervisory levels were as follows:

Lagerführerin, Camp Leader
Oberaufseherin, Senior Overseer
Erstaufseherin, First Guard
Rapportführerin, Report Leader
Arbeitsdienstführerin, Work Recording Leader
Arbeitseinsatzführerin, Work Input Overseers
Blockführerin, Block Leader
Kommandoführerin, Work Squad Leader
Hundeführerin, Dog Guide Overseer
Aufseherin, Overseer

It's worth noting that the notional career progression for female SS auxiliaries was largely illusory and most female guards remained mere overseers for the whole of their service. Nor was movement between

camps encouraged and most of the women allocated to Stutthof remained on the camp's establishment until 1945.

Training was originally a fairly lengthy and arduous process becoming rather less so after 1944. Recruits were toughened up and subject to gruelling indoctrination because they were expected to become callous and harsh towards those they would be guarding and to follow the pitiless approach espoused by Theodor Eike when the first concentration camp system was trialled at Dachau. However, they were encouraged to form sexual liaisons with their male SS colleagues which was never a disciplinary offence.

In consequence of their training, many more of the *Aufseherinnen* exhibited even more sadistic conduct than all but the worst of their male equivalents and it seems likely that this was the case in practice at Stutthof as elsewhere with female guards even more feared than SS men. Certainly the charges levied against female guards by surviving Stutthof inmates in 1945 seem to bear this out.

Personnel files recovered from Ravensbrück contain the names of twenty-two women, all with the rank of *Aufseherin,* listed below who served at Stutthof:

BECKER, Elisabeth (b. July 20 1923 Neuteich) Transferred Stutthof September 11 1944
BEILHARDT, Erna (b. February 7 1907 Neuteich) Transferred Stutthof September 18 1944
BERGMANN Ella (b. April 17 1923) Transferred Stutthof September 11 1944
BLANK, Elfriede (b. April 17 1923 Tiegenhof) Transferred Stutthof September 11 1944
BORK, Gerda (b. April 25 1922 Danzig-Ohra) Transferred Stutthof September 11 1944
BOTHE, Herta (b. January 8 1921 Teterow) Served Ravensbrück, Stutthof & Bergen-Belsen
BÖTTCHER (née BRÜCKNER), Hermine (b. April 26 1918 Wustung) Served Lublin-Majdanek, Neurohlau & Stutthof
BRILLOWSKI, Steffi (b. April 23 1916 Klosterwalde) Transferred Stutthof September 11 1944
BUKOWSKI, Rosemarie
CLAUSEN, Beate
GAZZA, Anna
HÜBNER, Erika (b. June 27 1921 Wiesau) Served Ravensbrück & Stutthof
HULSCH, Ilse
ISAAK, Ella

KAMINSKI, Erika (b. January 22 1920 Braunschweig) Denial she served at Stutthof contradicted by evidence placing her there September 6 1944
KLEINSTÜBER, Ruth
KOLLWAIN, Käthe
KRETSCHMER (née SCHÜTZE), Elisabeth
MÜLLER, Martha. Served Stutthof and Bruss-Sophienwolde
MUNZEL, Anneliese (b. April 23 1916 Strassburg) Served Ravensbrück & Stutthof
REPSCHLÄGER, Gretchen (b. October 1 1922 Lunow) Served Floßenbürg & Stutthof
WISOTZKI, Johanna (b. August 1919) Served Stutthof and promoted to Oberaufseherin at Bromberg-OST

Forty-seven Aufseherinnen trained at Stutthof itself and they were deployed as part of a total of 150 women serving the main camp and its sub-camps under the command of Oberaufseherin Anna Scharbert who had been promoted to after serving at Ravensbrück.

Other names of female guards can be found from the post-war Polish trials including the highest ranked female guard tried for Stutthof offences, *Oberaufseherin* Gerda Steinhoff. A former housemaid, Steinhoff was born in Danzig in 1922 and immediately before the war worked as a cook and then a tram conductor. She married in 1944 and had a baby before going to Stutthof as a *Blockführeri* in the woman's camp. She was quickly promoted and assigned to work at the Danzig-Holm sub-camp from 1st October, moving on to the Bromberg-Ost sub-camp at Bydgoszcz on 1st December where for ruthless devotion to duty she was awarded a medal. Steinhoff fled before the Russians arrived but was arrested on May 25 1945, tried and condemned to death for acts of sadistic abuse.

Of the Stutthof *Aufsherinnin*, the most lenient sentence was passed on Herta Bothe, who received only ten years imprisonment and she was released early from prison on 22nd December 1951 as an act of clemency by the British government. Born in 1921 in Teterow, Mecklenburg-Schwerin, Bothe worked from the age of seventeen in her father's small wood shop, then in a factory, and then as a nurse. In September 1942 she was recruited to work at Ravensbrück concentration camp for women and after a four-week training course was sent as an overseer to Stutthof where she allegedly inflicted brutal

beatings earning the nickname *The Sadist of Stutthof.* Wherever she went, Bothe literally stood out. She was six foot three inches tall (1.91 metres) and unlike most others wore civilian shoes rather than the officially issued black jackboots. Bothe's last posting by *Oberaufsherin* Steinhoff was to Bromberg-Ost from where she was sent to guard a death march to Auschwitz ending up at Bergen-Belsen until the camp was liberated on 15th April 1945. Had Bothe been tried other than by the British and in particular if she had been on trial in Poland, it seems likely that she would have received a death sentence given her reputation at Stutthof. In her defence she claimed that although she had struck inmates with her hands for camp violations like stealing, she never beat anyone other than with her bare hands and that she had never killed anyone. It appears she was believed by the court even though a Bergen-Belsen survivor claimed to have witnessed Bothe beating a Hungarian Jew named Éva to death with a wooden block while another stated that he saw her shoot two prisoners for unknown reasons. To be true that would have meant she had circumvented the rule that Aufseherinnen were never permitted firearms.

Another who was ultimately executed was Wanda Klaff. Born Wanda Kalacinski to German parents in Danzig in 1922 she worked in a jam factory before marriage in 1942 when she became a housewife, Klaff later went back to work as a streetcar operator until 1944 when she became a guard at the Stutthof satellite camps of Praust and Russochin. She fled the camp in early 1945 but on 11th June was arrested by Polish officials and survived a bout of Typhoid Fever in prison to stand trial. Accused of prisoner abuse, she was one of the few who effectively admitted her offences: '*I am very intelligent and very devoted to my work in the camps. I struck at least two prisoners every day.*' She was still only twenty-four when she was executed on July 4 1945 as was her colleague, Jenny Wanda Barkmann.

Barkmann was from Hamburg and like Klaff and many of the other Stutthof *Aufseherinnin* joined up in mid-1944. In her short career she was accused of extreme brutality, even beating prisoners to death and

making selections for execution in the gas chamber. Her severity and looks earned her the nickname *The Beautiful Spectre.* Barkmann fled before the arrival of the Russian army but was arrested in May 1945 at a Danzig railway station. On trial she treated the proceedings with disrespect, giggling periodically, flirting with the prison guards and arranging her hair while witnesses gave evidence. Her death sentence is perhaps less surprising than that for some of the others tried alongside her.

Ewe Paradies was twenty-three when she reported as an *Aufseherin* at Stutthof in 1944. She was allocated to the Bromberg sub-camp in October for four months, returning to Stutthof in January 1945. In April she absconded after accompanying a prisoner transport to Lauenburg in April 1945. At her trial Paradies was accused of ordering a group of female prisoners to undress in the freezing cold and then dousing them with ice cold water, beating them if they dared to move. She was also accused of killing prisoners in other acts of personal brutality for which she was sentenced to death.

Elisabeth Becker, a former cook, was born in Danzig in 1923 and joined the League of German Girls in 1936. She worked for the firm of Dokendorf in Neuteich, where she was employed until 1941, when she became an agriculture assistant in Danzig. She was called up for *Aufseherin* training on September 5 1944 and was then assigned to work in the Stutthof women's camp where her tasks included selecting women and children for the gas chamber. Becker fled the camp on January 15 1945 and went back home to Neuteich where on April 13, she was arrested by the Polish police. Her trial with other former *Aufseherinnin* and Kapos began in Danzig on May 31 1946 and she was one of ten defendants sentenced to death. Appeals for a pardon were refused by the Polish President, Bolesław Bierut and she was hanged on July 4 1946.

Erna Beilhart was born near Danzig in 1907 which made her comparatively old to be trained in the autumn of 1944 as a *Hilfsaufseherin,* an auxiliary female guard. She served at Stuuthof for

only three weeks from the 18th September to 11th October and then attended an overseer program for six weeks after which she moved to the satellite camp at Heiligenbeil. On January 20 1945 she accompanied the evacuation to Königsberg where she performed nursing duties on injured German soldiers as a member of the German Red Cross. Eventually she returned to the main camp at Stutthof, was captured by the Russians and tried for maltreatment of prisoners, receiving a sentence of five years' imprisonment.

The SS guards alone could not have controlled the vast number of inmates within concentration camps like Stutthof. Instead they relied upon an intermediate level of supervision and discipline provided by selected inmates and as the historian, Karin Orth, famously observed, *There was hardly a measure so perfidious as the SS attempt to delegate the implementation of terror and violence to the victims themselves.* The practice they were implementing was deceptively labelled prisoner self-administration - *Häftlings-selbstverwaltung* - but the stark reality was that they were practising a form of *divide and rule*, pitting inmate against inmate in their individual struggles for survival and, in so doing, were viciously multiplying the level of brutality within the camps.

A kapo was a prison functionary – *Funktionshäftlings* - commonly selected from among the criminal elements imprisoned in the camp and at any given time up to 10% of the camp population were kapos or *oberkapos* ranked by the level of duties they fulfilled. Thus a barracks leader – *Blockälteste* - was responsible for the discipline within a whole block, a room leader – *Stubenälteste* - ruled a room within a barracks block supposedly overseeing hygiene and de-lousing as well as reporting or punishing disobedience to the rules and a work foreman – *Vorabeiter* - supervised the performance of an external work detail.

Kapos were well rewarded. They were exempt from physical labour and abuse, given private sleeping quarters, allowed warmer civilian clothing and given extra rations as long as they performed their responsibilities to the satisfaction of the SS but their position was

precariously balanced and demotion was a constant threat often equating to a death sentence. As Himmler explained in a speech he gave on 21st June 1944. "The moment he becomes a kapo, he no longer sleeps with them. He is held accountable for the performance of the work…so he must drive his men. The moment we become dissatisfied with him, he's no longer a kapo, he's back to sleeping with his men. And he knows that he will be beaten to death by them the first night."

Kapos were often even more vicious than SS guards and five of the Stutthof kapos, Tadeusz Kopczynski, Waclaw Kozlowski, Josef Reiter, Franciszek Szopinski and Alfred Nikolaysen, were executed in 1946 for their treatment of inmates. Another, Marian Ziełkowski, a 44 year old from Wyrzysko, who enforced discipline using a wooden bat and rubber baton and admitted under questioning that administering beatings gave him pleasure escaped sentencing for his crimes, dying in his cell in August 1945 of a heart attack.

As the Lithuanian survivor Vladislovas Telksnys observed: "Officially it was Germans who ran things, but most of the beatings we took came from Poles. Germans knew how to wash their hands, they handed over all management to Polish inmates. Our wardens were fellow prisoners. Nasty, cruel people. One killed his own brother in Stutthof."

Other kapos curried favour and support from inmates by handing out rewards such as food or exemption from labour details and there were a minority who tried to balance the expectations placed on them by the SS with a degree of humanity. The pragmatic bargain struck by the Kapos was explained to Father Henryk Malak and his fellow priests by their Stutthof kapo, an older, bony and sharp-featured Pole named Gánski. He said, "If I start yelling at you it's because an SS guard is near so for God's sake work faster." By way of contrast to Gánski's attitude, the female kapo, Gerda Herper's favoured expression was, "You will have to work till you croak,"

Finally, for the inmates to fear, there were the dogs. Initially Stutthof did not use guard dogs but in 1941 a new brick building was erected in anticipation of the need to accommodate dogs and their handlers at some future point and an initial quota of ten dogs arrived on 27th September 1942 courtesy of a Waffen-SS infantry unit.

By May 1943 the records show Stutthof having twenty pure bred animals, Alsations, Boxers, and Schnauzers, primarily deployed to prevent escapes from work details outside the camp although on occasion dogs were encouraged to savage a camp inmate either as punishment for some infraction of the rules or simply for sport.

The Stutthof Museum Guidebook laconically records that the smallest dogs at 26 kilograms weighed more than many a starving inmate.

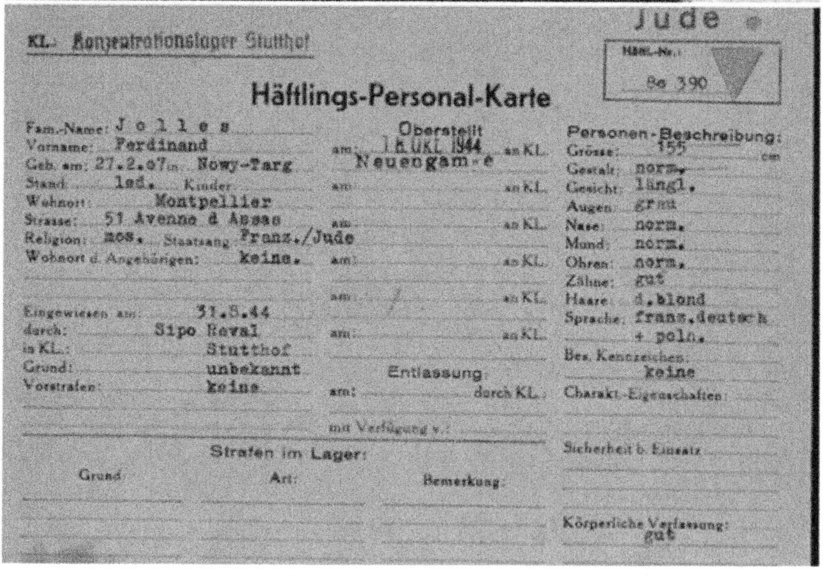

Jude

KL. Konzentrationslager Stutthof

Häftl.-Nr.: Be 390

Häftlings-Personal-Karte

Fam.-Name: J o l l e s
Vorname: Ferdinand
Geb. am: 27.2.07 in: Nowy-Targ
Stand: led. Kinder:
Wohnort: Montpellier
Strasse: 51 Avenne d Assas
Religion: mos. Staatsang. Franz./Jude
Wohnort d. Angehörigen: keine.

Eingewiesen am: 31.8.44
durch: Sipo Reval
in KL.: Stutthof
Grund: unbekannt
Vorstrafen: keine

Überstellt
am: 1 K UKL 1944 an KL. Neuengamme
am: an KL.
am: an KL.
am: an KL.
am: / an KL.
am: an KL.

Entlassung
am: durch KL.:
mit Verfügung v.:

Personen-Beschreibung:
Grösse: 155 cm
Gestalt: norm.
Gesicht: längl.
Augen: grau
Nase: norm.
Mund: norm.
Ohren: norm.
Zähne: gut
Haare: d.blond
Sprache: franz.deutsch + poln.
Bes. Kennzeichen: keine
Charakt.-Eigenschaften:
Sicherheit b. Einsatz:
Körperliche Verfassung: gut

Strafen im Lager:

Grund:	Art:	Bemerkung:

Top: Line up of Stutthof Guards
Bottom: Prisoner Identity Card of Ferdinand Jolles

Max Pauly and his wife

Himmler visiting Stuttof

Max Pauly introducing Himmler to his senior staff

The rabbit hutches

Aufseherinnen in training
(Photograph courtesy of the Ravensbrück Memorial)

Aufseherin Herte Bothe in British captivity

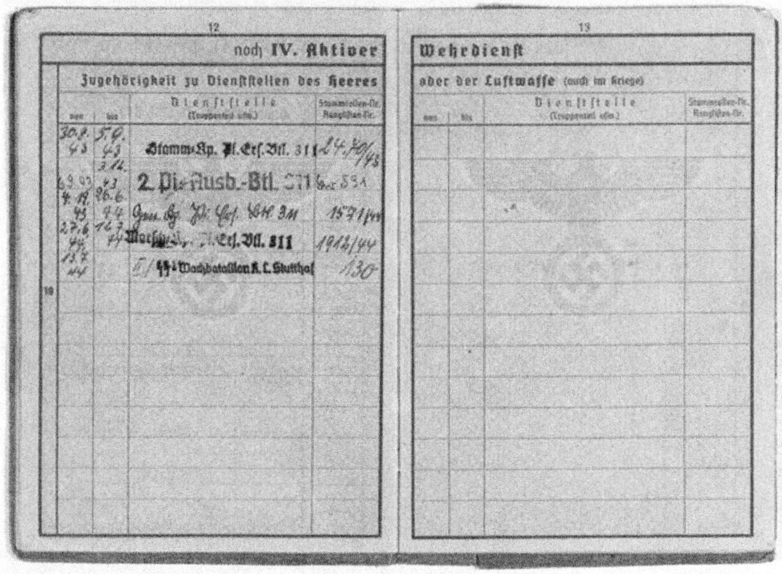

12 | 13

noch IV. Aktiver Wehrdienst

Zugehörigkeit zu Dienststellen des Heeres oder der Luftwaffe (auch im Kriege)

von	bis	Dienststelle (Truppenteil usw.)	Stammrollen-Nr. Ranglisten-Nr.
		Stamm-Kp. Pi.Ers.Btl. 311	
		2. Pi-Ausb.-Btl. 311	
		Marsch-Kp. Pi.Ers.Btl. 311	
		SS-Wachbataillon K.L. Stutthof	130

Wehrpass for Stutthoff guard Johann Liebig

Round up of Warsaw citizens forb deportation to Stutthof and elsewhere 1944

Paul Werner Hoppeb

Irmgard Dirksen (later Furchner), Hoppe's secretary at Stutthof

Odilo Globocnik

Trawniki Guards

PART 6
CAMP LIFE

THE TRADITIONAL PICTURE of inmates arriving at their assigned concentration camp in railway cattle cars has limited application to those sent to Stutthof. There were arrivals by rail but this involved a tedious transfer onto the local narrow gauge system from Teigenhof and more commonly transports involved fleets of open top trucks. Others completed much of their journey by sea.

Thus Max Kaufmann (Prisoner no.96046) travelled from Riga to Danzig on 6th August 1944 on the S/S Bremerhaven as one of a consignment of Latvian, Lithuanian, German and Czech Jews. At Danzig they were transferred into a convoy of small boats and carried along the coast, ending the journey with a march to and through Stutthof's Death Gate.

Another such arrival a month earlier in July 1944 was Phillip Maisel, a self-trained Jewish auto-motive repair worker who arriving in Danzig from Estonia by sea had to undertake a harsh two-day march along the coast to Stutthof for which no food or water was provided by his SS guards.

It became accepted custom that each group of new arrivals entering the camp through the main gate, the so-called Death Gate, was met by an SS officer. Zbigniew Raczkiewicz recalled being addressed thus: "From now on you are no longer a person, just a number. All your rights have been left outside the gate- you are left with only one and that you are free to do – leave through that chimney."

Newly arrived prisoners were grouped in the square in the Old Camp where they sometimes waited a day or longer, irrespective of the weather or time of year. Prisoners were reportedly beaten before they were entered on the camp register although beating of prisoners was prohibited by regulation towards the end of 1943. Inmates were then required to strip on the camp square, to hand over all personal possessions to the camp stores, records were made of personal details and any money credited against each prisoner's name. This was followed by the shaving of the head for both men and women, body-

searches for hidden valuables, a bath and then issue of camp clothing and a prison number..

To assist with disease control, a period of quarantine followed lasting between two and four weeks. The prisoners did not work whilst in quarantine but drilled in the morning supervised by the block or barracks chief.

Once the quarantine period ended each inmate was assigned to a barrack and also to a work commando. Sleeping quarters comprised three tier wooden bunks with paper mattresses and pillows stuffed with wood shavings and cotton blankets. Over-crowding commonly resulted in each bunk having three or four occupants.

Once female prisoners started arriving at the camp, the SS applied a very particular indignity to them. On arrival and periodically afterwards they were made to submit to gynaecological examinations. These were conducted in public in front of other male prisoners as well as guards.

The early Polish inmates at Stutthof wore their own clothes with lage crosses daubed on the back in paint. The clothing was thin and striped and in place of their own shoes, the inmates were issued with hard wooden clogs.

Exceptions were made for some classes of prisoner such as the Danes who wore civilian clothes and the Norwegian policemen who wore their own uniforms.

By the time Dora Rabinowitz reached Stutthof the days of rank and file prisoners wearing their own civilian clothing were long gone. "They said: *Anziehen* (get dressed) These were the striped horror clothes. If anybody had put dress with nails on the inside on you, that's what it would have felt like. They scratched you to pieces. You didn't have fat on you, at least I didn't. It scratched and made my skin bleed. That's what you put on. Over there is a row with what they called shoes. They were wooden soles with flat boots. Nobody cared what size you needed. You put those on and you went. All I kept

looking for was where are the others - my sister and mother. That was my total worry. We walked out and obviously the shoes that I had were such that it took a lot of attention after the war, orthopedic gadgets and help to stretch the toes because the shoes had been too small."

As the camp organisation became overwhelmed by the number of new arrivals in the second half of 1944, uniforms again ceased to worn. They were simply no longer readily available.

For the few weeks from mid-1944 that Phillip Maisel was detained at Stutthof, he wore "...a mismatched combination of short shirt, long trousers and a short woman's coat." His great good fortune was to be able to shame a fellow Jew who had been issued with Maisel's French army boots into returning them.

The eighteen-year-old Masha Gertler, arrived at Stutthof wearing an old black dress, a shawl around her shoulders and worn out shoes full of holes which before long she had to tie together with string. She wore those clothes for the ten months she was in Stutthof.

When the official sequential count of Stutthof inmates began there was no tattooing of numbers on the arms of prisoners as at Auschwitz nor at first the issuing of numbered patches to be sewn onto uniforms. Instead prisoners were each issued with a piece of cardboard bearing their camp number which they had to have with them at all times and they were supposed to memorise.

As in other camps, however, prisoners were eventually required to wear a colour-coded cloth triangle. Green triangles identified civil criminals, red triangles were worn by political prisoners, violet triangles denoted religious grounds for imprisonment, pink triangles stood for sexual perversion (not merely homosexuality but also paedophilia and other criminalised sexual inclinations), and black triangles were issued for those accused of anti-social behaviour and excessive drunkenness. The triangles of German citizens were plain whilst a letter identifying nationality was worn in the centre of a triangle issued to any of the scores of different nationalities of

prisoners who ended up in Stutthof. In the early years of the camp the yellow Stars of David worn by Jewish prisoners were far less common than they were to become after 1943. Even more of a rarity were triangles bearing three concentric circles. These identified repeat offenders who had been released from Stutthof but subsequently re-arrested since sentences at Stutthof were indeterminate with no hope of release except in the case of civil prisoners and some political arrestees.

For breakfast and supper the prisoners received a piece of bread with a tiny portion of margarine or jam, supplemented with a mug of ersatz black coffee while dinner was a bowl of thin soup made from turnip, carrot or cabbage scraps.

The issue of rations is one of the factors which demonstrate that the distinction some have made between concentration camps and extermination camps is wholly artificial. If a human male requires 3,000-4,000 calories a day to perform heavy manual labour, a regime which allocates a mere 1800 calories and in fact delivers merely 1000 calories is conducting a process of deliberate starvation.

'Food in the camp was appalling. Not unlike in other camps, we were fed cabbage glob without a trace of meat. They'd give us some bread, all soaked. .*(Vladislovas Telksnys).*

The war against hunger was a greater danger to most prisoners than anything else the SS perpetuated. It sapped all their energy and made them vulnerable to any and all diseases and illnesses prevalent in the camp. Worse still it tended to have the effect of rendering prisoners semi-comatose and uncaring of their fellow human beings, animals who who would steal food or any possessions which could be exchanged for food from anyone else simply to survive.

Those who coped best were those who who weren't alone in the camp. Small informal communities of common interest, usually based on geography or nationality, formed to safeguard each other, to nurse and feed the sick and most important of all to keep alive the spark of a hope that there would be life beyond their existence in

Stutthof. The SS whether deliberately or unwittingly sometimes encouraged such factional loyalties by allocating new groups of internees en masse to specific blocks but on other occasions, new arrivals were simply scattered through the camp and unless lucky enough to find themselves among comrades, those prisoners' chances of lengthy survival in the camp were slim. Group survival was possible; individual survival far less so

The barracks at Stuuthof were as previously described of basic construction, built without floors on packed bare earth. Their internal furnishings were equally basic. Roman Halter described just how basic they were; "Stutthof was not like Auschwitz, it is true, but it was hell nonetheless. We had to sleep two to a narrow bunk. Bugs from the bunk above kept dropping on our faces as we slept, and we were covered in bites from the lice and fleas."

Dora Rabinowitz described the living arrangements she endured in even more graphic terms. "We were first in a barrack together. Most of the barracks were a wooden stable. You've seen that, three people to a bunk. In the center there were four bunks. The horse blanket, the gray blankets that we called horseblankets were so rough. In any case, you got one to a bunk. You do me a favor and tell me how you share that, three people to a bunk. Nobody knew how to share it. The number of inmates decreased. People died like flies. We were again faced with this lack of water, lack of lavatories. There were latrines right over in the fields. They were just holes in the ground. You couldn't see in the dark. You were afraid to fall into them. It was slippery especially when the winter came and it all froze over. You got a mug of coffee. I always say this black water that was called coffee and after that you saved some to wash yourself. You have very good intentions at first. You really think you are going to rinse your mouth. Dental hygiene is very important. It wasn't then because you actually need the fluid in your body. So cleanliness goes to hell. Food you haven't got that would sustain you. After the first couple of days, you were being lined up to go to work or by that time, some looked

worse again and so the number got smaller. It was again right, left, right, left..."

Roman Halter again; "The morning roll call was at 7.15 a.m., but the block leaders would switch on the lights at 5.30 a.m. and literally within seconds we had to be out. Anyone who lingered was beaten with a stick. In our frail and starving condition, it was hard to recover from such beatings. We were made to wait outside for an hour and a half in the freezing Baltic winds with nothing on but our striped pajamas. The only way to beat the cold was to form a human oven by clustering together in groups, depending on each other, rotating rhythmically left and then right and then left again, stamping our clogs to keep our feet warm. Sometimes the kapos would charge at us with sticks to break us up, so we would wait for them to go and then start again. Anyone excluded from the human oven was doomed, and even with it people were getting sick and dying off."

Roll call was taken again at the end of the day so in addition to the work inmates undertook, they endured hours of standing around in the bitter cold at the behest of their kapos and the SS.

Stuthof not only had to be built and extended, it had to be maintained and it was the inmates who were required to perform all such tasks however unsuited their skills and state of health might equip them to do so.

Prisoners at Stutthof were required to work in allocated groups called kommandos. Each kommando was led by a kapo drawn from trusted prisoners and such kapos could be even more brutal than the SS guards.

Camp work included construction and maintenance, camp administration, clothes mending, cooking and, for women only, cleaning the Kommandantur. Other specialist roles were available carrying out joinery, painting, shoe-making, saddlery and lock-smith and gun-smith workshop tasks. These were coveted tasks because they were performed indoors and sitting down.

Stutthof's worst work kommandos were employed in clearing terrain for camp expansion. These groups cleared the land of trees, dug sewers and trenches, did drainage work, erected fences and built camp roads. Allocation to such a work commando on the rations available was akin to a death sentence.

Other internees worked in a camp brick factory and greenhouse as well as the vegetable garden and tending the rabbits being bred for their fur.

The working day was usually from six or seven o'clock in the morning until between five and seven o'clock in the evening, with an hours break for a lunchtime meal which was taken back in the camp for those engaged nearby. On Sundays, the prisoners worked only until mid-day.

For six or seven months of the year before the ground froze, there was a considerable demand for field labour in the vicinity of Stutthof and its sub-camps. The backbreaking work involved hoeing, planting, weeding and harvesting two main crops, potatoes and sugar beet as well as oil-seed rape and root vegetables.

As with other businesses around Stutthof, many of the farms were owned by Mennonites who showed little Christian charity in their often harsh expectations of the slave labourers they paid the camp authorities to hire. The Mennonite owner of one of the larger estates near Grenzdorf was SS-Scharführer Fritz Friese who personally selected prisoners from Stutthof to work for him and treated them so viciously that he came to be known as the Lord of Death and Life.

The major exception to Mennonite ownership was the *Gut Wederhof*, a manor house with a farm and brickworks run directly by the SS from April 1942 to which daily details of Stutthof prisoners were sent.

The harsh treatment of agricultural labourers was not always due to the farmers themselves however. The Stutthof Kapos supervising the work sometimes took great exception to farmers who showed common humanity. The Mennonite village of Tiege was one of the

communities using a contingent of 120 female Stutthof inmates in 1943 or 1944 to bring in a crop of rape-seed oil. Werner Klaassen vividly remembers the attitude of their kapo, a German Jew, who insisted that there be no fraternising with his charges and raised a huge argument when Klaassen's father gave the workers breakfast before they were sent out to the fields. The Kapo threatened to remove all the workers from the Klaassen farm and even to have Klaassen's father removed to Stutthof himself.

Slave labourers from Stutthof were also engaged in industries established within the confines of the camp, nearby in Stutthof and Stegna and in the vicinity of Stutthof's many sub-camps.

Some manufacturing concerns were SS-owned businesses such as the complex of three brick-built halls erected in 1943 next to the camp for the production of armaments. Known as the Deutsche Ausrustungswerke (DAW) by 1944 two of the employing about 120 prisoners in the production of Focke-Wulff aircraft parts. The third unit, a branch of F.Schiehau Gmbh of Ebling deployed another 100 inmates to produce motor parts, machinery and devices for the U-Boats of the Kreigsmarine. This work was deemed so important to the war effort and shifts were so much longer than the normal working day that those working there were exempted from roll call at the camp and had their meals ferried across to them at the factories.

Positions working with armaments were an obvious attraction for members of resistance movements even though the immediate penalty for sabotage was death. Nevertheless, Stutthof had a history of producing low quality firing pins which would shatter on repeated use.

Other Stutthof inmates were used in a synthetic petrol plant near Szczecin, in the Danziger Werft shipyard, in the brick-works of Hoppehill and at the Graniczna Wies quarry and contingents of Jewish prisoners inmates laboured on five airfields in East Prussia and building fortifications for the Todt organisation in Elbing and Torun.

In addition a Mennonite builder named Gerhard Epp, leased 300 Jewish slave laborers to build a new factory near the camp. Epp eventually took over as the general contractor to the SS in with responsibility for the construction of all camp buildings.

Skilled labourerers capable of supervising others were in high demand whilst intellectuals with no manual skills tended to be lumbered with the heaviest, most arduous tasks. Survival in the camp depended to a high degree on being allocated indoor work – kitchens laundry or in the administration. A sympathetic kapo or clerical worker in the kommandantur could literally save lives by allocating indoor duties to those most at risk of collapse. Polish political prisoners, including resistance members, understood this only too well and sought to place themselves in clerical positions where they could control record keeping and work allocation. Thus August Zagórski, formerly a postmaster in Danzig, ended up as the kapo in records keeping (where on occasion it was possible to exchange camp numbers and thus identities between recently deceased inmates and others) and Bruno Rekajski, who had served on the Polish General Staff at Pozńan, became the administrative assisistant for work party allocations. In that role he was able to exercise humanitarian judgments to help struggling inmates to survive. Aming those he helped was Balys Sruoga who credited Rekajski and Unterscharfführer Alfred Bublitz, who regularly brought him leftovers from the SS kitchen, with saving his life.

If lengthy roll calls, beatings for minor or invented infractions, mimimal rations and energy-sapping work were not enough, guards also engaged in other behaviours which can only be described as torture. Prisoners were made to lie on the freezing ground, hosed down with freezing water or injected with petrol.

Some female prisoners were subject to gynaecological examination as part of the process of admission to the camp and others faced sexual intereference from and rape by male guards and kapos under threat of punishment or death for non-acquiesence. Pregnancies did arise

but in low numbers as starvation stopped ovulation and menstruation. The guards ensured that any babies delivered alive did not survive.

Since barracks were single sex, some male kapos chose to maintain and protect one or more favoured young men as their assistants who shared their rooms and to some extent their authority.

What must be made clear at this point is that the demands of survival and in particular of acute hunger and thirst generated both acts of humanity and of otherwise atypical selfishness. Many in the camps would steal food at the least opportunity and the only way to combat such predatory behaviour was to band together. Frequently the most effective protection lay in tribalism. The Scandanavians tended to stick together as did Poles, priests and Jews. Their fiercest enemies were frequently not only the SS and their kapos but also desperate Russian and Hungarian prisoners-of-war. When humanity re-asserted itself however the consequences could be surprising in a place like Stutthof.

For example in December 1943, a Christmas tree was erected by the SS in the middle of the camp and covered in coloured lights. It had never happened before and never happened again.

The tree became a rallying point for SS guards and trusted criminals to carouse and drink around. Those who had no access to it chose another way of celebrating the season as the Danish prisoner Martin Nielsen, related. In the dark he heard deep and strong male voices. Their voices were clear in the cold night air. Polish prisoners sang as a choir one of the season's loveliest songs, of peace on earth. When he got closer he saw several hundred Polish prisoners standing by the barbed wire singing a Christmas greeting to the women in their barracks. When it died for a moment, the silence was broken by a an answering choir of female voices. The barbed wire could not stop the singing. Before long a chorus of Russian men were singing too and were answered by female Russian singers. Then there was silence for a moment.To Nielsen it felt as if the night had become holy.

Suddenly, the silence was broken by the beam of a spot light and a guard yelling from the watch tower "Get inside you lice infested, dirty swine dogs or I'll shoot."

Escape from Stutthof itself was never seen as a serious prospect. The difficulty for would-be escapees lay in the camp's geographical location as well as its physical barriers and guards. To the north lay only the Baltic coast and no prospect of stowing away on a ship other than in Danzig or Gydnia, an exposed trek westward through German occupied villages. To the south lay dense forest and pursued by dogs a man or woman on foot would be unlikely to get far. Then there were the barriers posed by the River Vistula and other significant water courses and tracts of marshy terrain.

Escape attempts when made were usually by the most desperate of inmates for whom a bullet in the back – shot while attempting to escape a work detail – offered a welcome release. It was also understood that escaping successfully would result in a terrible price – ten prisoners to be executed in place of each escapee.

By 1944 although a small number of prisoners, including Marcjan Czarnecki, Karol Viola, Stanislaw Jankowski and two unknown Englishmen, had escaped from satellite camps, nobody had ever successfully escaped from Stutthof itself. Wlodzimierz Steyer was determined to change that. The twenty-one year-old Pole, (Prisoner No. 35629) became the only man to stage a successful escape from the main camp.

He decided on a particularly brazen solution. He simply walked out of the camp, carrying a tool bag: "Acquaintances from Mokotow that just arrived in the camp told me what happened to the capital after the uprising had been suppressed. My urge to take revenge was growing. I was thinking about escaping again. However, it was sheer coincidence that helped me make the decision. One of the prisoners licensed to move among different working sites came to the delousing centre and told me how easy it was to go through the gate from the building site to the Jewish women's camp. I remembered

immediately carrying pots to this camp through a small gate, close to the kitchen.

"The plan was simple. I had to wait in the camp until the prisoners set off to work through the main gate, and then walk through the women's camp and hide in the unfinished buildings next to the delousing centre while everybody was returning to the camp for lunch. Leaving through the small gate I would not be counted so the number of prisoners coming back would tally with the number who had gone out. After a signal the sentry would come down and my road to freedom would be open. I needed to prepare quickly so that other prisoners would not hit upon the same idea. After two unsuccessful attempts with my companions, I decided that this time I would escape alone. I smuggled some plain clothes, a sack with fake tools and a piece of wire into the camp and received the address of a bakery in Nowy Dwor Gdański. I also got 45 deutschmark. I was ready. I weighed myself and my 76 kilograms assured me that I had enough strength to escape. My confidence was even greater when I found out from my friends working in the political department that Berlin had approved a whipping of 25 lashes as my punishment. I had nothing to wait for.

"On November 14th 1944 I arranged for another prisoner to cover for me in the relief gang while I stayed in the camp alone. I wore plain clothes under my camp uniform with distinct crosses, which in turn I covered with a trench coat no crosses painted on it. I also wore a black peaked camp. I had through the small gate with no difficulty. Once inside the barracks I was shocked to see rows of women in torn rags, their heads shaven, sitting against the walls and waiting for their turn to die.

"Pretending to be fixing something I slowly approached the gate to the building site. A bored guard did not even notice my leaving the women's camp. I walked round the square a bit, trying not to attract anybody's attention. When the prisoners were getting ready to march off to lunch I hid in one of the unfinished barracks. At 12 the trumpet

from the gate tower signalled that all the prisoners had come back to the camp. I still needed to wait while for the sentry to come down. All of a sudden I heard the sound of heavy boots walking behind me. I was in a room with one wall missing. I was motionless, on my own in an unenviable situation. If they had managed to catch me after the trumpet signal, they could have hanged me as I already had escape record and was attempting another escape.

"The footsteps of the guard came closer and closer. I briefly caught sight of him through a small opening. The guard stopped. There was a 12 centimetre wall between us. One more step forward and he would have found me. Every second was like an hour. After a while the guard turned around and his steps became more and more distant. Then I decided to leave the building and pretend to be a civilian foreman going to lunch.

"I passed the building site headquarters and a few SS-Men standing outside their barracks. Nobody took any notice of me as the trumpet signalled that all the prisoners were already eating their thin soup. Without haste I started walking up a small hill separating the camp from the road. From the hill I could see the whole camp, but I could also be seen. Suddenly I saw an SS patrol with dogs in front of me rushing to the canteen. I hid myself in a nearby wooden toilet, where I watched them go past towards the camp. Afterwards I left the toilet and tried to get to the road. Climbing a small forested hill I saw another SS platoon. I turned back to the camp and setting out on a semi-circular route I finally reached the road which took me safely to Stegna."

Neither the young nor the old did well in Stutthof. Nor those condemned to the heaviest forms of physical labour - exhaustion, malnutrition and ill-treatment by the guards saw to that. Those without the support of friends and peers discovered that isolation was akin to a death sentence - inmates ostracised by other prisoners, such as homosexuals, were far less likely to survive. Survival was the province of the strong - those prepared to subvert the regime, using

contacts in administrative positions to obtain less onerous, indoor work, to steal the food of other inmates, to become or befriend the Kapos, and at the most desperate times (as Thøger Thøgersen and several other Danish survivors have testified) to resort to hunting rats and even to cannibalism of the dead. From January 1945 when most of the camp population had been evacuated, a daily work party of Scandanavian inmates was sent out each day to scour the countryside for rotting potatoes and to try to catch loose and starving horses to be slaughtered to feed the main camp.

Survival it seems has little truck with the morality of normal existence. It requires a strength of will, an obdurate refusal to succumb to despair, and in the face of random violence from the SS and the risk of exposure to disease, at Stutthof it also required luck.

The length of prisoner stay in Stutthof varied greatly. A few old-timers such as Mieczyslaw Filipowicz (Prisoner No. 2676) imprisoned as one of the surrendering defenders of the Westerplatte, survived over five years there while other inmates were merely passing through en route to other work camps or to Auschwitz-Birkenau for extermination. Then there were lucky few on short-term sentences of defined length and men with friends prepared to raise funds to get them released.

Erika Mannheimer, a German Jew born in Bad Wildungen in 1923 had the not untypical experience of incarceration in eleven different ghettos and camps between 1941 and 1945. She and her mother, Lina, were among 20,000 Jews shipped to the Riga Ghetto of whom only 500 survived the Holocaust. Erika and her mother themselves lost over 80 family members. Until October 1942 Erika worked folding parachutes and also for the Luftwaffe laundry service. On one occasion she recalls cutting scraps of silk out of the parachutes she was packing to make new underwear. She was subsequently moved to other tasks in different concentration camps, avoiding the lethal transfer to Auschwitz-Birkenau. She arrived in Stutthof for four weeks in mid-1944 where she was overjoyed to be reunited with her

mother. Spells in satellite camps at Thorun and Korbern followed and there she was forced to help blow up bridges and dig anti-tank trenches to delay the Russian advance. She subsequently survived a death march back towards Germany, arriving at the Bromberg Concentration Camp to be liberated by Russian soldiers on 27th January 1945.

Another Jewish survivor, Leo Kuttner was arrested on 1st September 1939 and spent several months working in a shipyard and on a farm. Arriving at Stutthof in 1940 he was incarcerated there for four years, employed in upholstering furniture or in winter, if there was no productive work available, pointlessly carrying snow from one location to another. Deportation to Auschwitz as a street cleaner and to dig ditches occurred in 1944 but he avoided selection for extermination, survived a death march from Flossenburg and was liberated by the Americans in April 1945.

Many such Stutthof survival stories have been recorded in post-war memoirs mentioned elsewhere in this book but they include Helena Katz (Helen Lewis), a Jewish dance teacher born in 1916 to a German speaking family in Bohemia who passed through Terezin and Auschwitz before Stutthof from where she was liberated in 1945; Edmund Zoledowski born in 1900 was a violinist who performed at Stutthof for the SS being rewarded with cigarettes and the extra rations which no doubt contributed greatly to his survival; and Halina Strnad who was 17 when she arrived at Stutthof in 1944 and survived typhus, unlike her mother who died in her arms.

Concentration camp inmates working in typical aircraft parts factory at unidentified location

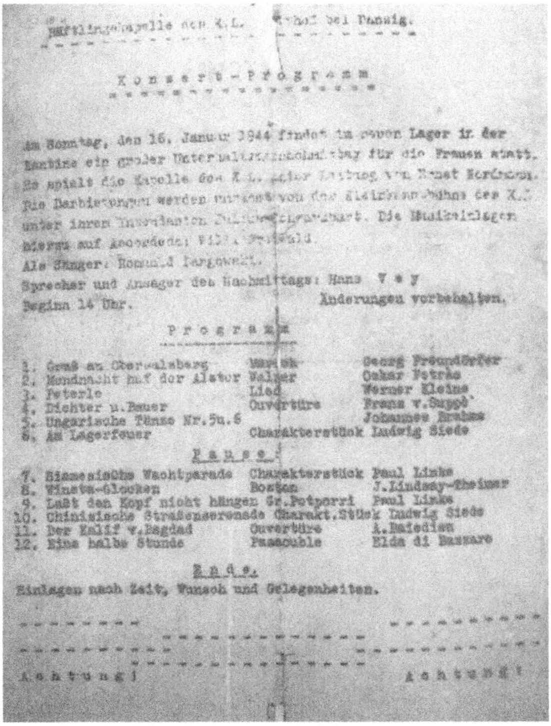
Häftlingskapelle des K.L. [illegible] bei Danzig.

Konzert-Programm

Am Sonntag, den 16. Januar 1944 findet im neuen Lager in der Kantine ein großer Unterhaltungsnachmittag für die Frauen statt. Es spielt die Kapelle des K.L. [illegible] von Ernst [illegible]. Die Darbietungen werden [illegible] von der [illegible] des K.L. unter ihrem [illegible]. Die Musikeinlagen [illegible] auf Accordeon: [illegible]
Als Sänger: Romuald [illegible]
Sprecher und Ansager des Nachmittags: Hans V e y
Beginn 14 Uhr. Änderungen vorbehalten.

Programm

1.	Gruß an Oberwalsberg	Marsch	Georg Freundörfer
2.	Mondnacht auf der Alster	Walzer	Oskar Fetrás
3.	Peterle	Lied	Werner Kleine
4.	Dichter u. Bauer	Ouvertüre	Franz v. Suppé
5.	Ungarische Tänze Nr. 5 u. 6		Johannes Brahms
6.	Am Lagerfeuer	Charakterstück	Ludwig Siede

Pause.

7.	Siamesische Wachtparade	Charakterstück	Paul Lincke
8.	Winsta-Glocken	Boston	J. Lindsay-Theimer
9.	Laßt den Kopf nicht hängen	Gr. Potpurri	Paul Lincke
10.	Chinesische Straßenserenade	Charakt. Stück	Ludwig Siede
11.	Der Kalif v. Bagdad	Ouvertüre	A. Boieldieu
12.	Eine halbe Stunde	Pasodoble	Elda di Bassaro

Ende.
Einlagen nach Zeit, Wunsch und Gelegenheiten.

Achtung! Achtung!

Stutthof Concert Programme

German propaganda poster in Polish depicting ideal of agricultural labour

The Mennonite Epp family – large scale employers of Stutthof slave labour

Epp machine shop in Stutthof

The barrier to escape posed by flooding on the Vistula (photographed by Otto Bruck)

PART 7
DISEASE AND DEATH

THE SQUALID living conditions for the prisoners held at Stutthof made the rampant spread of disease inevitable.Although the barracks huts contained washing facilities these were completely inadequate for the number of inmates and accessibility was limited by the minimal time allowed for dressing before roll call and the issue of such rations as constituted breakfast. In addition water shortages and the issue of scraps of soap was a wholly exceptional circumstance and the whole regime made a mockery of the fatuous clause in the regulations which required concentration camp inmates to maintain cleanliness and personal hygiene.

Overcrowding within barracks huts meant two or more sharing every bunk and the excess population sleeping huddled together like sardines in straw on the floor and that in turn provided the ideal breeding conditions for lice to thrive, populating the seams of the thin summer clothing or striped uniforms worn by inmates and ultimately enabling the rapid dissemination of diseases such as typhus.

Stasys Lal, the Lithuanian priest imprisoned in Stutthof, graphically described the scale of the problem. During their short lunch intervals, they would sit to conduct lice hunts, squashing each louse they found between both thumbnails. He laconically observed that "Eighty at a sitting was the average…"

Not only were the prisoners crowded together lice-ridden and filthy but most suffered from bowel conditions as a direct consequence of camp diet and diahorrea was an endemic problem especially given restrictions on the availability of latrines and that the single set of underwear issued to each prisoner was worn until it fell apart and then was seldom if ever replaced.

In such circumstances as these only extensive medical interventions could prevent epidemics and these simply did not exist. Instead the regime seemed designed to encourage death by natural causes as the means of removing the ill, the dependent and those suffering work-related injury and collapse from the camp population.

Just as the barracks themselves were never adequate to accommodate the numbers incarcerated at Stutthof, the hospitals provided were never sufficient to effectively treat the effects of malnutrition, the consequences of brutal slave labour and the scale of epidemics which came to dog the concentration camp not least because provision of hospital beds was based upon the ratio used by the Wehrmacht – 3 beds per 100 men in service.

The first infirmary established in 1939 was built with bunks for 30-40 patients. It was rapidly overwhelmed. Pneumonia, Pleurisy and frostbite were the commonest afflictions. All the inmates had to wear was the increasingly tattered summer clothing in which they had been arrested back in September and they were both labouring outside and then being made to parade for roll calls lasting hours at a time in the bitter conditions of a Polish winter. In addition there were kidney infections arising from poor diet and limb-shattering accidents on construction tasks.

The worst cases - those gravely ill or requiring surgery for example - were sent on the regular weekly or twice-weekly journey by truck to Danzig to be treated at the Staatlide Akademie Für Medizin. Selection for the privilege of such medical attention was however dependent on the goodwill of of SS-Hauptsturmführer Otto Haupt whose idiosyncratic judgements were seldom particularly influenced by the opinions of the Polish doctors working under him at Stutthof. For the cruelty underlying his selections for treatment or death, Haupt eventually received a twelve-year prison sentence from a court in Tübingen in 1964.

One of the transfers sent to the Akademie was a Pole named Anton Siniecki whose family were enabled to see him in hospital thanks to the humanity of a German orderly who sent them an anonymous postcard with the news of his injury. Like other Polish transferees to the hospital, he must have hoped that this was a precursor to release but that hope was never realised. All the surviving Stutthof patients

were sent back there and Siniecki died exactly a year from the date of his hospital discharge on 19th March 1940.

In March 1940 a new hospital barracks was created at Stutthof with 120 beds which still proved insufficient and the onset of a typhus epidemic in the spring of 1942 the hospital grew into a five unit institution with a total of 600 beds (which soon enough became over-crowded with over 1200 patients) - two units housed surgical cases, two more handled infectious diseases (including a ward dedicated to Tuberculosis cases) and finally there was an isolation unit. The group long together of patients into specialisms had one unforeseen consequence - it created wards which the SS staff declined to visit to avoid the risk of infection removing the prospect for those patients being selected for execution as unlikely to return to productive labour.

The medical facilities for Jewish inmates were even cruder than those for the rest of the camp. Attended by a handful of those who had been nurses in another life, almost completely lacking in medicines and equipment they provided no more than a temporary refuge in less crowded bunks than the main blocks. Only the seriously ill ever went to the hospital block and those either died or recuperated just enough to leave before the next periodic SS purge which would clear all the bunks, sending the occupants to the gas chamber or even directly to the crematorium to be burnt alive. Such purges occurred every week or two.

Masha Gertler, reached Stutthof, accompanied by her mother and sister, with a raging fever. Expelled from the Łódź ghetto the family had been in Auschwitz for a fortnight before being shipped in an arduous two day journey by rail box-car to Stutthof. A woman called Rozka, who appeared to be in charge of the barracks the Gertlers were allocated to, insisted Masha go to hospital where a Jewish nurse assured her she would be safely looked after for a few days, the SS having been just two days earlier. That assurance proved unfounded because guards arrived on Masha's third day in the block, turfed out

the volunteers and emptied every bunk in the place. The only survivor was Masha. Huddled down, the solitary occupant of one of the top bunks, she was miraculously missed.

Such was the medical kingdom inherited, once Stutthof was officially recognised by Himmler as a concentration camp, by the first short-lived Chief Physicians SS-Untersturmführer Dr. Werner von Schenk and SS-Obersturmführer Dr. Johannes Otto and by their successor from 28th April 1942 until the war ended in 1945, SS-Hauptsturmführer Dr. Otto Heidl.

Dr. Heidl was born in the Sudetenland, a region along the border between Germany and Czechoslovakia annexed by Hitler in September 1938, and he undertook his medical training in Prague. His induction into the SS came comparatively late - he was drafted on 14th February 1941 and his membership number was 328012. He served first at Auschwitz and Groß-Rosen where he gained a reputation as an implacable selector for death of patients unlikely to fully recover. It was a reputation he seems to have carried with him to Stutthof and traded upon so that underlings did not cross him and yet oddly his actions there were, by comparison to his previous exploits, far less cruel. In the long run it wouldn't matter because, placed on trial at Bochum in 1955, it was clear the evidence of crimes against humanity at Auschwitz would ensure his conviction and he committed suicide in his cell before his trial could be concluded.

Although the hospitals were run by the SS, and most of the orderlies (referred to as *Pfelgers*) who were employed to distribute medicines and food, valuable commodities in a concentration camp, were SS Non-commissioned officers, the actual work of tending the sick and injured fell to doctors and assistants who were mostly Polish although a Lithuanian, Dr. Antanas Starkus would also later serve with distinction. Since the day to day running of the hospital was delegated to Poles, sick and injured Stutthof inmates of German nationality would do almost anything to avoid ending up in their care. With some justification they feared that being tended by their country's enemies

would result only in their deaths. For Poles the fear of hospitalisation could be equally strong because they were well aware that periodically the SS would inspect the wards, marking down for removal and execution anyone deemed unlikely to be briskly returned to the camp workforce.

The earliest Polish detainees in Danzig included doctors who were to become the primary health professionals at Stutthof. They were a surgeon, Aleksander Witkowski, Stefan Kopczyński, Witold Kopczyński (transferred from Stutthof to Oranienburg-Sachsenhausen in 1941) Edmund Zieliński and the man who took charge of the treatment of infectious diseases, Stefan Mirau. Witkowski was the only one of them who survived the whole six years of the war in Stutthof as well as the death marches of 1945, being liberated by the Red Army at the village of Gęś near Lębork.

In March 1940 Stutthof gained three more medical assistants from Toruń. All three were qualified doctors; another surgeon, Józef Dębski, a gynaecologist, Bogdan Jasiński, and Julian Węgrzynowicz. More doctors arrived in the latter part of 1942 including Bolesław Kaczyński, Józef Roszkowski, Lech Duszyński, Anna Paszkowska, and Alfons Wojewski, while a Dr Kwiatkowski was sent to Stutthof in late 1944.

As well as an orderly (only a few of whom were trusted Polish or Czech inmates) each hospital block employed Polish cleaners (*Hausers*) but things changed in 1944 the reverses being suffered by Axis forces lead to the the German orderlies being called up for frontline service. Thereafter the hospitals were almost entirely managed by Poles and other prisoners.

Malnutrition and physical exhaustion combined with lack of basic hygiene and crammed accommodation had the inevitable consequence that immune systems were weakened and disease was endemic among the camp population including cholera and typhus. Typhus outbreaks kept occurring because the cause is bacteria carried

by the millions of lice within prisoner clothing which periodic delousings only marginally inhibited.

Dysentery and typhus were not the only major diseases to reach epidemic proportions within the camp. Another was tuberculosis which claimed the life of one of the Westerplatte defenders, a civilian employee of the Polish navy, Alojzy Januszewski, on 26th October 1942 after performing slave labour at Stutthof for nearly three years. The grounds for his continued imprisonment had been confirmed in a memorandum from the Gestapo in Berlin dated 23rd May 1940: *His conduct threatens the existence of our nation and the state, his anti-German attitude raises concerns that, if he is released, he will still work to further the Polish agenda.*

The camp as originally constructed was not anticipated to have a high mortality rate and no specific arrangements were made for handling corpses. Indeed initially the bodies of prisoners who had died or had been murdered were transported to Danzig and buried in common graves at the Zaspa Cemetery or, in a few cases, handed over to Danzig's Anatomical Institute.

The typhus epidemic of 1942 changed all that and presumably accounts for the building of the crematorium alongside a gas chamber in mid 1943.

During the typhus epidemic in 1944 the crematorium could not keep up with the number of bodies to be disposed of and a crematory pyre was set up to the north of the New Camp. The pyre was constructed so that there were alternate layers of corpses and logs or boards. The Soviet and Polish investigating officers in 1945 took this to be further evidence of genocide although it seems more probably the result of inability to cope with the death rate from disease.

Even the mass pyre was insufficient and the Jewish women's blocks became virtual graveyards with bodies dragged just outside or left on the hut floors where they had died.

From the earliest days of the camp deliberate executions did take place at Stutthof. Thus, on March 22nd 1940, 67 members of the Gdansk intelligentsia were shot outside the camp. The victims included postal workers, businessmen, priests, printers, journalists and lawyers, among them Anastazy Wika Czarnowski, former director of the Polish Post-Office, Pawel Rozankowski, an engineer from the Port of Gdansk Council, Franciszek Krecki, a Polish economic and social worker, Bronislaw Komorowski, Rector of the Polish church of St. Stanislaus in Wrzeszcz, Wladyslaw Pniewski, a teacher at the Polish Grammar School and Antoni Lendzion, an opposition member in the Free City of Danzig *Volkstag*.

Such executions required ratification from Berlin and then the means of execution was more commonly hanging than shooting. Some hangings reportedly took place in open view, presumably to deter others from acts of sabotage or escape attempts which led to the death sentence. Other condemned political prisoners were apparently hanged behind the crematorium.

Among those executed was Leon Fuz, one of the postal workers who fought to defend the Danzig Post Office from the Germans on 1st September 1939. He escaped the fate of most of his surviving colleagues who were tried as illegal combatants and swiftly executed by a firing squad commanded by Max Pauly. Unfortunately for Fuz, who had been transported to Stutthof, he was later recognized, a piece of ill-fortune which led directly to his death.

Another executed prisoner was an unknown Russian prisoner who attacked a young kapo called Ziehn with a hammer. Ziehn recovered. His assailant was hanged.

Some prisoners arrived at Stutthof already condemned to death for offences against the Nazi state. They did not officially enter the camp itself but were hanged or shot, again behind the crematorium. To some extent their non-inclusion in the camp's recorded arrivals and deaths bridges some of the gap between the camp's official death toll

and post-war estimates of those whom Stutthof proved a one-way journey.

Commonly when transports arrived from Gdansk carrying people earmarked for execution, they were taken immediately to underground cells in a small building at the side of the Old Camp where they were held pending shooting or hanging before the evening roll-call.

Krzysztof Dunin-Wasowicz, at Stutthof from May 1944, recalled the arrival of one particular prisoner: 'In the afternoon, when Ludtke wearing his ironic smile arrived at the Rapportabteilung with a card in his hand, we all knew what was to come. The condemned who had been brought to the Rapportabteilung waited about half an hour, then just before the roll-call Oberscharführer Chemnitz and Oberscharführer Foth arrived and took them towards the crematorium. There they were either shot in the back of the head, or hanged.'

One of themajor dichotomies to be found in comparing the SS regulations applicable to concentration camps to the way in which many SS guards conducted themselves, lies in the use of violence against inmates.

The process of inmate dehumanisation by the SS was so advanced that spitting on prisoners, kicking and beating them were routine occurrences. However worse than that was the fact that SS guards at Stutthof felt they were licensed to kill individual prisoners at will for trivial offences or none at all.

Conversely camp administrators and Kommandants were under instructions from Oswald Pohl's department to minimise wastage of useful labourers and the regulations forbade the use of direct violence against prisoners. Even flogging was supposedly to occur only at the orders of the Kommandant and even then all such sentences had to be cleared with Berlin before they were carried out. Such regulations seldom, if ever, resulted in punishment for any Stutthof guards breaching them.

One clear loophole lay in the fact that guards could be rewarded with a week's leave for preventing escapes. Hence Leo Kuttner witnessed SS guards snatching prisoner headgear, tossing it away and ordering the unfortunate owners to collect it. Obeying those orders resulted in being shot *trying to escape.* Not following such orders resulted in potentially fatal beatings. Similarly there are examples of watchtower guards using their rifles to shoot an inmate to alleviate their boredom by *preventing an escape.* Thus on 20th August 1940 a Danzig merchant, Max Bless and another inmate called Hans Lachman were both shot by guards from watchtowers.

Sometimes the guards would simply hurl a prisoner against the electric fence instead according to Asia Shindelman (Prisoner No. 54138). A Lithuanian born in 1928 and deported aged sixteen to Stutthof on 25th July 1944, she was giving evidence in 2021 at the trial of Irmgard Furchner.

Another such murder was conducted by Dr. Heidl's assistant, SS-Hauptscharführer Otto Haupt. Haupt was by reputation both vicious and greedy. Professor Fyodor Soprunov (Stutthof number 23506) said of him; "He was greedy, thoughtlessly greedy for anything at all. He used to take anything he could lay his hands on in the camp: clothes, bread, gold teeth extracted from prisoners. He took these things to his house in Tiegenhof." On one occasion he bundled a newly arrived prisoner onto the barbed wire fence and shot him for attempting to escape. He had been told by a kapo of a rumour that the man had swallowed a diamond. Haupt then forced the Lithuanian Dr. Starkus assisted by Professor Soprunov to conduct a post-mortem, carefully washing the intestines. The search failed to flush out the supposed stone to his considerable fury.

On other occasions a guard simply beat a prisoner to death within the confines of the main camp although the death certificate issued for such victims needed to be issued with a falsified cause of death to cover up the actuality. An example may be found in the case of Natan Steine whose death is recorded on 20th August 1940 from a *Crushed*

chest. It seems probable that he was the victim of a regularly conducted SS *toughening up exercise* in which a victim was required to lift a boulder and carry it to an arbitrary point from which he was then ordered to pick it up again and take it back to the starting place. Collapsing under the weight of the boulder meant a beating or being savaged by dogs with death the inevitable result.

Other examples from the camp records include Doctor Karp Makarewicz-Minc, previously a prisoner at Stalag 1B Hohenstein, who was murdered on February 21st 1944, four Jewish prisoners-of-war transferred from Hammerstein killed on March 15th 1944 and eight prisoners, four of them Jewish, hanged on January 16th 1945.

In fact recovered death certificates include several suspicious *suicides.* On 6th May 1940: six Jews *Committed a suicide by hanging themselves.* Almost certainly they were forced to hang each other by SS guards. The same thing happened with six more Jewish inmates on 16th June, less than six weeks after the first recorded incident.

Other inmates were murdered by kapos; evidence of such murders led to the imposition of the death penalty for several Stutthof prisoner functionaries after the war. Further instances of deliberate murder of inmates by guards whether by beating, strangulation or shooting were also evidenced in post-war trials, especially of the most brutal female Aufseherinnen.

Murders also took place within the infirmary of those deemed unlikely to recover sufficiently to be fit to work again. Horrifically these were murders carried out by medical staff who used lethal injections to stop a patient's heart. This was the fate of Josef Salomonovic's Czech father. The Stutthof museum records state that the substance used was phenol and certainly phenol was used for this purpose in other camps.

Dr. Węgrzynowicz (Stutthof number 9230) later wrote an account of killings by the SS within the confines of the hospital; "The SS men finished off patients. I soon realized that Haupt, who managed the hospital on a regular basis, and his assistants killed patients. There

was a fat Oberscharführer, I do not remember his name, and also a Scharführer. Both of them drowned patients in the bathroom, but this method of mass murder was so to speak demanding and inefficient. That way he could kill two, three, five patients a day, which was not many."

From 1942 until 1944 the Germans applied a quicker method of eliminating unwanted patients using injections of phenol or other corrosive substances intravenously or directly into the heart. The process was known as *'needling* among the prisoners and reached its zenith in period from August to October 1944.

Dr Węgrzynowicz stated in his account of Stutthof that Dr. Heidl, who commonly treated him as partner whose opinion should be considered, would, during a ward round, select on average seventeen patients a day from the internal diseases unit to receive a lethal injection. Heidl however never included the TB or Typhus wards in his rounds - he was too afraid of being infected himself. The selected patients were taken to a washroom "...where there was a small table with already filled syringes on it. After Heidl had injected phenol into the prisoner's vein, he ordered him to take off his shirt and lie down in the corner on the cement floor. As it took the shot a few minutes to start working, the patient had enough time and strength to take off his shirt and lie down. And that's how it went. Heidl told each of these prisoners, one after another, to lie down on the pile of corpses..."

Dr. Heidl's sense of self-preservation was not in fact unjustified. Two of the original Polish doctors in the camp, Stefan Mirau and Stefan Kopczyński, both died of diseases they probably contracted from their patients in 1942.

Heidl's selections for euthanasia were not always injected by the man himself. Sometimes that task fell to his assistant, Otto Haupt, who seems to have performed it with a certain relish. "Almost every day he beat up prisoners, and almost every day he killed some," said Professor Soprunov.

Finally it must be acknowledged that murders were also perpetrated by other inmates most commonly as an unintended consequence of beatings to secure the surrender of hoarded bread or in self-defence. It doesn't after all take that much to kill a half-starved human being.

A gas chamber was only finally built at Stutthof in mid 1943, its intended use being for delousing prisoner clothing, lice being carriers of typhus.

Elsewhere though gas chambers were beginning to be used for the extermination of human beings. The blunt truth is that mass shootings proved too prone to produce among the SS personnel carrying them out the forms of breakdown which later in the century would come to be labelled Post-Traumatic Stress Disorder. Himmler himself having witnessed such massacres was personally distressed and set his staff to finding an alternative. They explored carbon monoxide poisoning before discovering the efficacy of the pesticide Zyklon-B. Gassing had two significant advantages. Firstly it distanced those in control of the operation from what they were doing while further de-humanising the victims and secondly much of the process of extermination could be delegated to prisoners, to kapos and work details, who could be charged with packing those selected to die into the gas chambers and clearing out and cremating the bodies afterwards leaving the SS merely the tasks of supervision. Such delegation had never been possible when the means of death had been machine guns, pistols and bullets.

Unsurprisingly after Rudolph Höss arrived to instruct Stutthof's guards in the use of Zyklon B, mid 1944 saw the first culling of Jews deemed too sick or unwell murders in the small gas chamber at Stutthof. There remains significant academic dispute as to how much use was made of the gas chamber and how many people could be squeezed into it (see Part 9 of this book) but the fact that it was put to lethal use is undeniable. Thus, Nesse Grodin who was transported to Stutthof in 1944 gave evidence after the war that at Stutthof Jews were not gassed if they were between the ages of 15 and 45 or were

older but still capable of working. A girl herself, Grodin was looked after by older Jewish women: *They would make me stand tall and pinch my cheeks to get the blood flowing in them when the Germans came around to take sick people away to the gas chambers…If you looked sick, there was a good chance you would be chosen to die.*

From the evidence given by Grodin and others it is clear that the purpose of the gassings was to remove unproductive mouths and unnecessary cost from the equation. The purpose was brutally economic and its contribution to Hitler's *Final Solution* of the so-called *Jewish problem* almost certainly incidental.

Toilet and washing basins in New Camp

Stutthof today clockwise from top left:
1.Railway track and gates
2.Gallows
3.Barrack huts
4.Kommandantur

Narrow guage railway wagon at Stutthof

Stutthof today clockwise from top left
Infirmary; Gas Chamber; Bunk beds

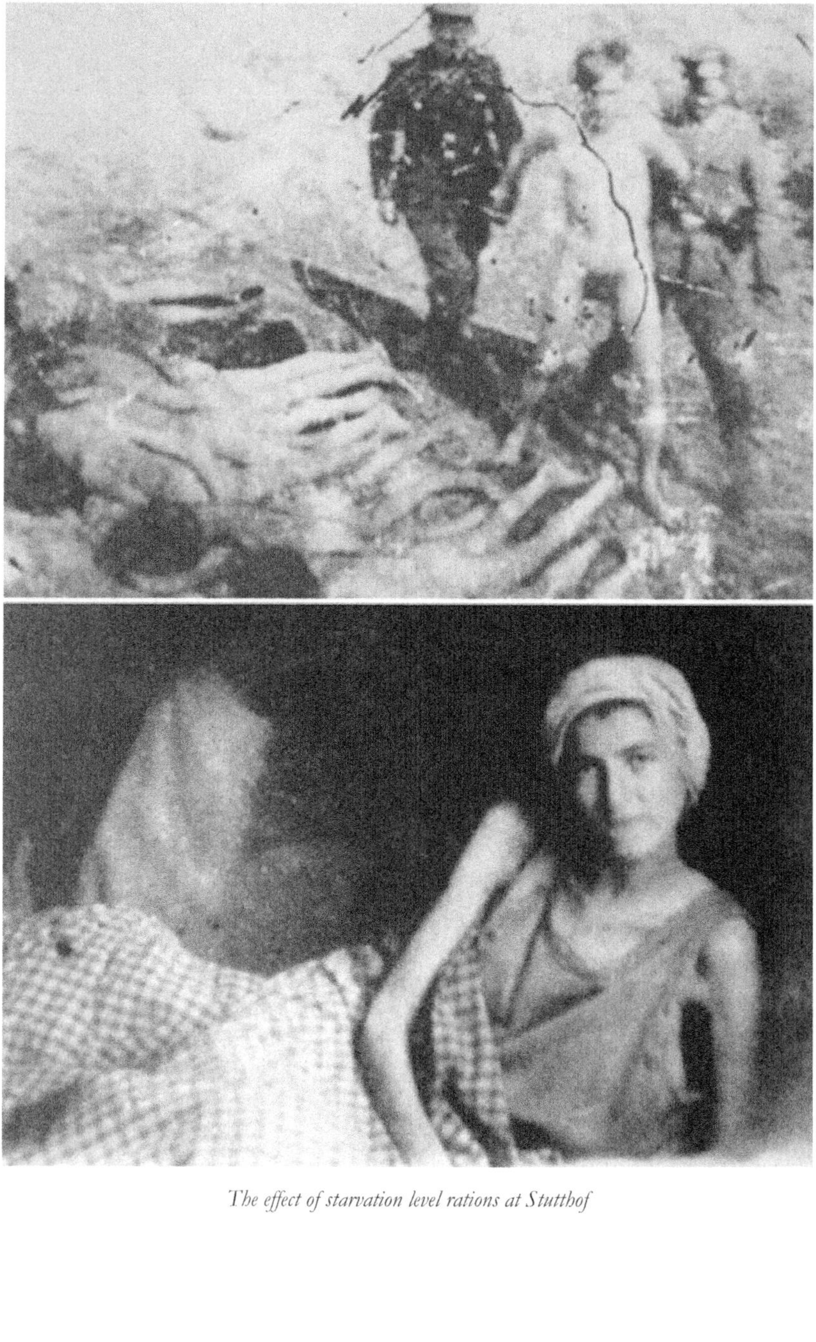

The effect of starvation level rations at Stutthof

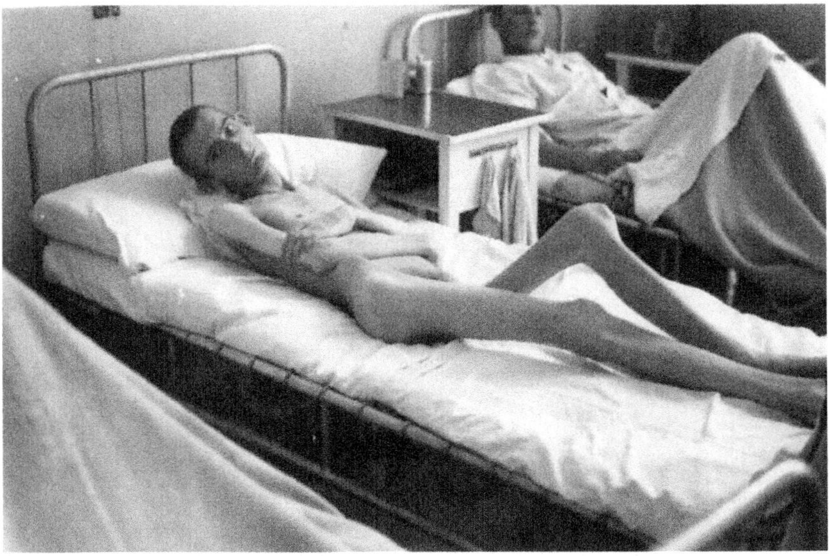

Stutthof survivors, Denmark 1945

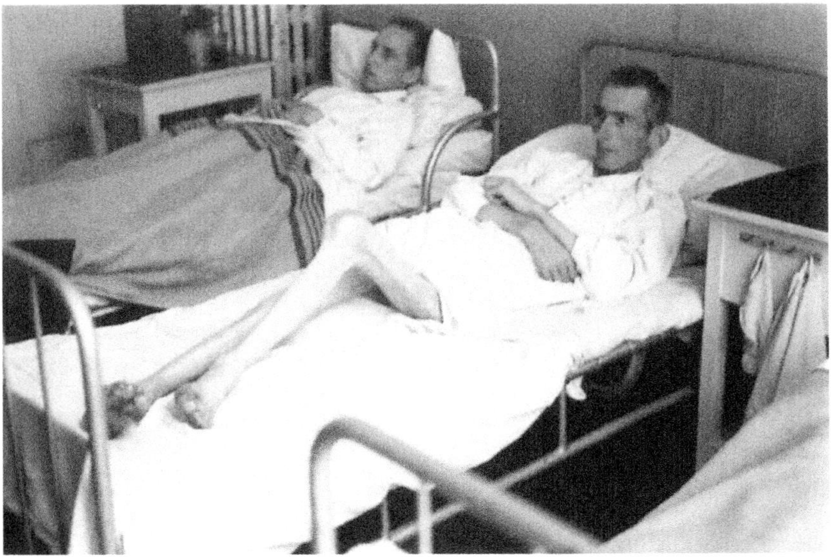

PART 8

1945

IN THE DEPTHS of a bitter Polish winter, plans were under consideration which would result in a nightmare trek for Stutthof inmates away from the concentration camp towards the German border along rough, snow-covered roads, in inadequate footwear – battered and ill-fitting wooden clogs, disintegrating civilian shoes or in some cases nothing at all – wearing thin camp clothing, already half-starved after months or years in ghettos and as slave labourers, marshalled by guards using rifle butts to enforce movement and willing to end with a bullet the life of any laggard or straggler unable to continue.

Stutthof was not the only concentration camp planning such an evacuation and the tracks and roads the refugees would have to traverse would inevitably be shared with hundreds of thousands of other holocaust survivors, retreating military personnel and displaced persons, mostly women and children, slowing progress to a crawl. There was never a clearly achievable end destination in mind for any of the camp evacuees. Whether they ended up somewhere or whether they died would be a matter of chance, dictated by the speed with which allied forces were advancing to cut them off, food shortages, the breakdown of communications with the SS guarding them and indeed the willingness of the guards to see through such orders as they were given or instead to desert, abandoning their charges or even murdering them first.

Such were the foreseeable and inevitable consequences of the order Kommandant Paul Werner Hoppe would be signing.

From 6th August, 1944, with the Red Army advancing into Latvia, the Germans began to evacuate the camp at Kaiserwald, moving the inmates by forced march to Stutthof and shooting those deemed unfit to make the trek as well as every Jew under 18 and any Jew ever convicted of any offence, no matter how minor. The evacuation to Stutthof was complete by September 1944 but it was obvious that eventually Stutthof too would be overrun.

In the face of the Russian advance into Poland, Albert Forster, as Gauleiter of Danzig and Fritz Katzmann, Military District Police Leader decided Stutthof should be evacuated.

Hoppe signed the formal evacuation order, *Einsatzbefehl No 3*, on January 25th, 1945 at 0500 hours and the evacuation began an hour later. The initial destination was a sub camp of Stutthof situated near Laurenburg some 87 miles (140 km) to the West.

The main evacuation from Stutthof had been expected to last seven days. 25,000 prisoners in nine columns started the march with the last two groups leaving the camp on the 26th January:

"When they fell down, a blow with the rifle butt tried to lift them up. They were too weak to continue the march; some of these falls were their last falls. An SS-man's kick removed the body to the side of the road. Sometimes one kick was enough or one knock with a rifle butt in the face, to finish the life. We hardly passed Stegna, when one prisoner fell down; after that others were falling."

Another survivor who lived to give evidence of this death march was Lily Mazur Margules from the Riga Ghetto who had been deported in 1943 to the Kaiserwald camp and then transferred to the Duenawerke labour camp. Her next deportation was by sea to Danzig and on to Stutthof where she was allocated work in a satellite camp. Her ultimate journey away from Stutthof on foot early in 1945 ended at the Prussian town of Krumau and she described "Conditions of extreme cold resulting in the legs of some women becoming frozen stiff so that the could only topple face down into the snow never to rise again and not even requiring an SS guard to expend a bullet on them."

The march actually took ten days, not seven and food had only been issued for two days. The columns marched on through snow drifts in inadequate shoes and clothing and with SS guards murdering anyone who fell behind. Most of the survivors reached Lebork where, in March 1945, they were liberated by the Red Army.

Aged 16, Nesse Grodin was on the forced march with a group of around 1,000 other female prisoners; "When the Soviet army liberated the group on March 10, 1945, only 200 women, including me, were still alive…"

At the same time as the evacuation of the main camp commenced, some 13.000 inmates, who were mainly female Jews of Polish and Hungarian extraction, from the Stutthof subcamps at Heiligenbeil (Mamonowo), Jesau (Juschny), Seerappen (Ljublino) and Schippenbeil (Sępopol), were sent on a similar forced march eastward to Königsberg (Kalingrad). Many died en route in the harsh winter conditions and it proved impossible to get into Königsberg because the city was already under siege by Soviet forces. Some were forced to return to Stutthof but for up to 3,000 women the march ended in a brutal massacre on the white Baltic sands of the beach at Palmnicken (Yantarny).

The SS initial intention was to wall up the women in the tunnel of an old amber mine. They were frustrated by the resolute opposition of the local Volkssturm officer, Hans Feyerabend.

Feyereabend's position was undermined by a majority of the local inhabitants who simply wanted the problem of the concentration camp inmates to disappear. The women were then marched onto the beach to be forced into the ice-cold Baltic Sea and machine gunned to death.

Helpless to stop this tragedy happening, Hans Feyerabend took his own life while German villagers were to be disappointed in their wish to see the problem disappear because the bodies kept being washed ashore and ten weeks later an irate Russian commander, who happened to be Jewish, forced the local inhabitants to bury all the corpses themselves.

There were survivors of the massacre but less than 200 of them and all but 15 of them subsequently died before the war came to an end that May.

The Germans were by early 1945 desirous of removing all the concentration camp inmates back into Germany rather than leaving them as living or silent witnesses to their war crimes. The propaganda value to the allies of the scenes which greeted the liberators of Bergen-Belsen had already been noted by Himmler who appreciated that evidence of what had happened in the other labour and death camps would both stand in the way of any negotiated peace agreement to end the war and stiffen the allies resolve to bring high-ranking Nazis to trial once victory over Germany had been secured. His somewhat ambiguous orders to all Kommandants left most of them in little doubt that they were to destroy all written records, to evacuate as many prisoners as possible it was possible to and to kill all those who couldn't be moved.

At Stutthof many incriminating documents were burnt and manufacturing equipment transported away from the camp. Other camp records were boxed ready to be removed but as it transpired in the eventual chaos as the last of the SS guards attempted to flee before the Soviets arrived, much of it ended up dumped in roadside ditches and was later recovered.

The Kommandant, Paul Werner Hoppe chose to leave Stutthof with most of his senior staff on 4th April heading for Schleswig-Holstein where he would take over a new concentration camp at Wöbbelin

On Hoppe's departure, command passed to SS- Hauptsturmführer Paul Rudolf Ehle with SS-Rottenführer Franz Kukklau as his deputy and 40 SS-guards assisted by the trusted German prisoners making up a unit of Lagerpolizei (camp police).

Hoppe's final orders to Ehle were to surrender the camp with the rest of the prisoners but since that order was at odds with subsequent demands from Himml;er that all the camps be totally liquidated, Ehle was given reinforcements in the form of a battalion of German Gendarmerie to enable the evacuation of all transportable prisoners. It was understood that any too ill would be eliminated, and the rest of the records burnt with all the buildings.

During the latter part of March 1945, the Russians besieged Danzig from the south. On 28th March they took Gotenhafen (Gydnia) and on 30th Danzig. Stutthof was completely cut off on land. The only reason the Soviets had ceased to advance westward much beyond Marienburg (forty kilometres east of Stutthof) and had chosen instead to encircle the narrow coastal strip between the camp and Danzig was because of the region's plethora of lakes, marshland, forest and moorland coupled with deliberate flooding caused by the Wehrmacht's opening of drainage lock gates and sabotaging of dykes and watercourses, rendered the terrain unsuitable for the tanks in the vanguard of the Red Army. That isolated pocket of land between Marienburg and Danzig remained the sole Polish territory still in German hands when the war formally ended with German surrender on the 9th May.

Stutthof's population by March 1945 largely comprised prisoners from sub-camps who had been part of unsuccessful marches eastward and those deemed too sick to be included in the January evacuation. For them the only option left lay in maritime evacuation across the Baltic Sea.

An initial evacuation of Stutthof prisoners from the sub-camp at Gotenhafen (Gdynia) took place on 25th March 1945 and involved two coastal cargo vessels; the S/S Elbing and the S/S Zephyr which transported 618 inmates to Hamburg for transport to Neuengamme. It was not a notably successful operation because whilst 700 prisoners set off to march to the port, nearly 100 escaped to go into hiding in the town. Few of those who arrived at Neuengamme or its sub-camps survived the war and a number were among those who were forcibly embarked on the ill-fated SS Cap Arcona at the beginning of May.

With the increasing urgency of addressing evacuation of the main camp, the SS had only one final plan that might work. The pocket of German held territory including Stutthof stretched as far as Nickelswalde (Mikoszewo) at the mouth of the River Weichsel (the Wisła). The significance of Nickelswalde, some fourteen kilometres

from Stutthof, was two-fold. It contained a ferry crossing as a potential embarkation point, and it was the western terminus of the narrow-gauge railway serving Stutthof giving the option to transport at least some inmates by train rather than marching them all along the coast.

With precious little preparation the final evacuation began simply because it had proven possible to assemble four river barges, four tugboats and a naval motor vessel on the Weichsel which could, at a pinch transport, 5,000 people across to the tip of the Hel Peninsula where Hel itself was the last coastal port still in German hands after the fall of Danzig and Gotenhafen. Even if the inmates could not be transhipped at Hel to larger vessels, in fair weather conditions the barges, however unsuited for non-coastal voyages, might just make it further along the coast to Lübeck in German waters. There were, however, no guarantees.

Stutthof to Nickelswalde 25th-26th April

The first leg of the evacuation, led by Feldgendarm Hauptmann Otto Schmidt (a military police officer not an SS guard), took place on 25th April and was undertaken as a forced march for most of the inmates with a minority assigned a place in one of several massively overcrowded narrow-gauge railway wagons. Each of the selected 3,000 or so prisoners was supposed to receive travel rations comprising half a kilogram of rye bread with a portion of margarine and a small piece of smoked horse meat. That was little enough but distribution was patchy and some received nothing at all. Unsurprisingly, given that most of the prisoners were starving and there was always the fear of assault and theft by another desperate inmate, most consumed everything the moment they received it, condemning themselves to a subsequent fast of unknown duration.

The train arrived at Nickelswalde after midnight and the prisoners were disembarked to spend the night penned into a meadow to sleep in the open air. They were joined the next morning by the marching

columns and left to their own devices while the guards took turns to avail themselves of beer and food at a nearby Gasthof. No more food was issued to the prisoners but they were able to drink from the river and some took the opportunity to wash themselves. The day was not without incident, however. Finn Dahlin, one of the Norwegian Policemen from Stutthof, saw a young Jewish women, who was seeking privacy to urinate, shot in the head because she had come too close to the trench at the rim of the meadow area and another shot beside the river embankment by SS-Untersturmführer Schmidt and SS-Oberscharführer Ewald Paul Foth. Other Norwegians intervened to prevent further murders by persuading them to cease fire.

Come the evening, the prisoners were loaded onto three river barges; the *S/B Wolfgang*, the *S/B Vaterland,* and the *S/B Klaus*. The owner of the *Wolfgang*, Gustav Wicht was trying to take his whole family to safety so the adult members formed his crew and the guards comprised about twenty SS and Gestapo and perhaps forty Police Gendarmes.

Nickelswalde to Hel: The Wolfgang, Vaterland and Klaus

The first three river barges to depart from Nickelswalde transporting Stutthof prisoners, SS guards and Feldgendarmerie, cast off soon after 03.00 hours on 27th April. The *S/B Wolfgang* (carrying around 1,000 inmates closely packed into the vessels nine holds) towed by the *S/T Adler*, the *S/B Vaterland* (carrying around 1,000 packed inmates) towed by the *S/T Bussard*, and the *S/B Klaus* (carrying about 600 inmates) towed by the *S/T Danzig* were sailing the thirty-two kilometres at night to avoid being bombed and strafed by Russian fighter planes.

The conditions on the barges were cramped in the extreme. Hermine Schmidt described the situation on the *S/B Klaus* thus; "Below deck in the cargo holds reigned complete chaos. People were literally lying on top of each other. Filled with lice, starved, seasick and in despair

they trampled each other down with their feet."

The voyage to Hel took two hours and they arrived by 06.00 to be disembarked in the teeth of an attack on the harbour by Russian aircraft. Marched some three kilometres into the forest to a barbed wire enclosure, it soon became evident that this was no safe haven either as an air attack was soon underway on an adjacent German artillery position. Stray ordinance killed ten Stutthof inmates and wounded several more. The chaos was exacerbated by the guards shooting and killing others who in understandable panic were trying to flee.

In the event, the surviving prisoners were fairly swifted marched back to the port and re-embarked on the three barges. There were no available larger vessels onto which the Stutthof prisoners could be transhipped and the officer in charge of this phase of the Stutthof evacuation, SS-Oberscharführer Heinrich Enns, decided that should leave the increasingly dangerous port of Hel and set off westward again in convoy with eighteen other ships, including naval escorts and vessels carrying German refugees and wounded soldiers. They were heading for Lübeck via Swinemünde (Usedom). Enns placed himself aboard either the *S/B Klaus* or its tug, the *S/T Danzig*. It would not prove the wisest option.

The S/B Klaus

In dense fog, the *S/T Danzig* lost touch with the rest of the convoy and its barge, the *S/B Klaus*, ran aground off the tiny island of Greifswalder Oie, not far from a naval station and the infamous V2 rocket testing facility at Peenemünde. Attempts by the *S/T Danzig*, to salvage the barge were abandoned because it started to break up. And the fearful occupants were left aboard until a naval vessel could arrive. When it did the guards (around forty Feldgendarmes and perhaps twenty SS and Gestapo) were evacuated and 473 prisoners on the barge were taken onto rubber floats and towed to land. The

prisoners too weak to climb out of the barge's hold were left as were two prisoners who fell into the sea.

The Stutthof evacuees were given fresh water at the naval station but if they thought that would conclude their sufferings they were wrong. They were next loaded onto a barge carrying a perilous cargo of ammunition and torpedos and ferried to Lauterbach where, according to Oberscharführer Heinrich Enns, food was made available by the fire brigade. What Enns failed to clarify was that the food was for the guards; the prisoners stayed hungry for the next two days. They were also left without anywhere to shelter from the wind and rain. Sympathetic civilians tried to help but when a local baker brought them a consignment of bread, it caused a stampede and mass fights as the guards tried to regain control of the situation. During the chaos twelve prisoners were shot and killed and up to 130 prisoners were believed to have escaped into the local woods or found shelter with local civilians. Among the escapees was a Pole called Władysława Adamczyk who remained in the forest until the area was liberated by the allies on 6th May. Many others presumably did the same.

Those prisoners still in captivity were then loaded onto another barge, the *S/B Breslau,* which was moored up in Lauterbach's harbour, and the *S/T Danzig* arrived to tow them on onward, their journey recommencing on 3rd May. The barge was much larger than the *S/B Klaus* so the prisoners were far less cramped and one of the cargo holds contained a load of sugar which some prisoners may have been able to access. Although fairly clean, the *S/B Breslau* was in very dilapidated and unseaworthy condition and the risk of it taking on water and sinking must have been ever-present in the prisoners' thoughts, tortured as they were by the continuing lack of drinking water. A short stop late morning at Saßnitz yielded no supplies and they set off again.

By now new fears for their fate were circulating because Antoni Kawalek, a Polish Stutthof inmate had spotted crates of dynamite

aboard and become convinced that orders had been given to scupper the barge at sea. Another Pole, Pjotr Mierzejewski, was spreading a different story – that they were to be cast adrift on the Baltic – and an elderly Jehovah's Witness called Sister Malenke was saying that the captain had admitted he had orders to drown them all but was not intending to do so. None of the more lurid predictions came to pass – instead the Captain had set a course for Denmark but the danger was far from over because the barge was leaking badly and soon a red distress flag was run up the mast.

Oberleutnant Paulo on the *S/T Danzig* , was able to establish radio contact with the Danes and by agreement with an accompanying German naval vessel on the morning of 5th May he made landfall, bringing the wallowing barge into the tiny harbour at Klintholm on the island of Møn.

Some of the SS guards and Feldgendarmarie disembarked to seek help to continue their voyage to Flensburg but were peacefully persuaded by local civilians to leave the beached barge and its cargo of Stutthof evacuees in Klintholm.

The surviving evacuees were in a sorry state. As described by a local journalist, Gert Munch, "Everyone was in rags. Everyone was very ill with tuberculosis, pneumonic plague, typhus, and every single prisoner suffered from terrible nutritional diseases. Everyone had lice. The creatures in cargo hold no. 1 were not able to stand on their legs. They were lying like a heap of dying animals, who had once belonged to the peculiar homo sapiens. The stench down there was hard to endure for a fresh human being."

Another journalist, Otto Walsted, was less factual in his observations but more graphic. "The first thing the Møn population saw of the inmates of this Baltic Sea ark as they flocked at the landing site, was a cluster of dirty, ragged and indescribably skinny human beings who faltered up the chicken ladders from the deep darkness of the ark and tumbled against the railing in a confused and struggling mob."

Apart from widespread diarrhea, many of the evacuees had Typhus. Some had left Stutthof with it; others had contracted iten route to Denmark. The doctors at Klintholm also found multiple cases of tuberculosis, phlegmona, ulceration, hunger oedema and pleurisy while great many prisoners had gaping and infected wounds to to their scalps, limbs and backs from being beaten, whipped and kicked.

The Danes behaved with impeccable charity. Dr. Rasmus Fenger, Niels Rosenkrantz, the local resistance commander, Dr. Mortensen and his wife who was the chairperson of the local Red Cross immediately established a committee to provide milk, bread, potatoes, drinking water and fresh clothing while the sickest prisoners were taken to hospital in Stege. Volunteers bathed and disinfected them and set up temporary sick bays in the Klintholm Beach Hotel and all the nearby villages as well as latrines for prisoners remaining on the barge until accommodation on land could be found. Undoubtedly the actions of Klintholm's residents saved many lives which would have increased the final death toll for the voyage dramatically.

The Stutthof evacuees who arrived alive on 5th May were carefully counted by the Danes; there were 370 survivors and nineteen of them died shortly after they were liberated. This accounting doesn't quite tally with the 473 stated to have survived the shipwreck of the *S/B Klaus* but either that number was wrong or the Germans over-estimated the number said to have escaped during the chaos at Lauterbach. Either way the death toll was probably in the region of a hundred of those male and female prisoners evacuated on the *S/B Klaus* - mainly Poles and Russians prisoner but including fourteen German Jehovah's Witnesses - who had, until evacuation, survived the Stutthof Concentration Camp.

The manner of death on the sea legs of the evacuation provided ample evidence of the cruelty the SS and Gestapo only too often delivered. They included those who fell overboard and either drowned or were used for target practice by the guards, those shot at

the ship's railings or thrown overboard as they tried to urinate over the side, deaths from drinking seawater and those dying from infectious diseases who were hauled onto the barge's hatches and thrown overboard in the night whether still alive or dead.

Hel to Neustadt – The Wolfgang and The Vaterland

Many of the 2,000 evacuees loaded at Hel onto the *S/B Wolfgang* and the *S/B Vaterland* on 28th April were the very same prisoners from Stutthof disembarked a few hours earlier.

The owner of the *Wolfgang*, Gustav Wicht was trying to take his whole family to safety so the adult members formed his crew and the guards comprised about twenty SS and Gestapo and perhaps forty Police Gendarmes.

The *Wolfgang* took about half the evacuees from the dockside, mainly Poles, Russian POWs and Jews (most of them women), but was allocated all the higher staus prisoners. They were placed in the first three holds on the *Wolfgang* where preferential treatment comprised somewhat less cramped surroundings and occasional access on deck once the vessel was underway. These higher status prisoners were mostly Scandinavian with an additional ten male and two female Lithuanians. The Scandanavians comprised 223 Norwegian policemen, plus 9 male and 5 female civilians, 25 male and 6 female Danes (all left wing activists), and 72 male and 7 female Finnish sailors all of whom had received Red Cross parcels of food before departing Stutthof and thus might have been attacked by the other starving prisoners if they had not been placed in separate holds.

The *Vaterland* was crewed by four members of the Kreigsmarine, the German navy and to control the prisoners carried Gendarmerie-Hauptmann Otto Schmidt with 40 of the 130 East Prussian Police Gendarmes under his command as well as a similar number of SS guards and Gestapo functionaries as the *Wolfgang*. That the guards managed to cram between 900 and 1,000 prisoners onto the *Vaterland* was quite a brutal feat given that it still carried a partial cargo of

machinery and scrap iron which had never been a priority for unloading.

On 30th April the barges reached Stralsund. The port was full and the city already virtually cut off by the Soviets so there were no supplies of food or water to be had for the prisoners and the convoy set off again that afternoon, heading for Warnemünde which they reached on the next day, 1st May, but they were turned away and proceeded to Travemünde near Lübeck.

While moored up at the Travemünde shipyards, a handful of prisoners got over the side but were soon captured and handed over to the German military authorities. Two Norwegians took advantage of the fracas to get themselves across to the *S/T Adler* hiding aboard while tug left the barges on a further unsuccessful mission by its captain, Franz Sell, to get supplies. In Lübeck they completed their escape and managed to reach the sanctuary with the advancing British army.

The 2nd May found the barges and their tugs anchored off Neustadt in the naval harbour where those evacuees able to walk were permitted to exercise which in practice meant to scavenge among the rubbish for anything that resembled food until marines gathered to force re-embarkation.

A number of large vessels were already assembled in the bay, many of them already holding concentration camp evacuees, and the *Wofgang* and the *Vaterland* now had orders to moor up alongside one of them, the *S/S Thielbeck*.

Gendarmerie-Hauptmann Otto Schmidt engaged in negotiations with Heinrich Bertram and John Jacobsen, the respective captains of the *Cap Arcona* and the *Thielbeck*, to take his prisoners on board one or both of the larger ships. Discussions foundered on the insistence that food rations be provided with any transferring prisoners and Schmidt's deputy, Gendarmerie-Oberleutnant Thiel, had failed to get the harbor commandant to provide any. Eventually Schmidt simply abandoned the barges, taking the Wicht family to the *S/T Bussard*,

also now moored to the *Thielbeck*, to spend the night and using the two tugboats to transport the Gendarmes, SS and Gestapo guards over to the Neustadt U-Boot-Schule where both warm food and comfortable beds awaited them. The prisoners were left with only their Kapos to supervise them.

At 01.00 on 3rd May, Hauptmann Schmidt lost any last chance he might have had of resolving the impasse his prisoners faced in the bay: Kreigsmarine officers confiscated both his tugboats stranding all the *Wolfgang* and *Varterland* guards on dry land.

In this vacuum the Scandinavian prisoners took charge as one of the Danes, Hans Christian Staub described; "We were a number of Danish sailors and we grasped the initiative right away. All moorings were cast loose, and a couple of men were put in the row-boat in order to keep the barge adrift and keep it to the wind. We collected all the blankets we could get and held them into the wind."

The *Wolfgang* began to drift away from the *Thielbeck* but the wind was slight and even with four Norwegians and a Finnish sailor on the oars rowing as hard as they could progress was infinitesimally slow. Seeing what was happening, Gustav Wicht managed to scramble back aboard his barge only to be taken hostage and locked up in his own cabin.

Meanwhile prisoners on the *Vaterland*, seeing what was happening on the other barge, followed suit, slicing the mooring ropes and using wooden boards to get the vessel drifting shorewards.

It took them between three and four hours to ground the barges close inshore on the beach at Pelzerhaken but it took a lot longer to get those prisoners capable of climbing out of the cargo holds off the barges because the rowing boat from the *Wolfgang* and another one found on the beach could each take at most six or seven on each trip. The result was a growing number of small parties of Stutthof prisoners roaming nearby gardens in search of vegetables and knocking on the doors of nearby houses, among them the young Finnish sailor, Aarne Kovaala.

Dora Rabinowitz from the *Vaterland* found milk and vegetables and returned to the beach to build a fire. Others brought water and started cooking soup.

The motley invasion of Pelzerhaken did not go unreported for long and news soon reached Neustadt's Bürgermeister, Ernst Reicher. He managed to raise the local leader of the Volkssturm Militia, Dr. Detlef Käselau, a dentist and former airforce officer, who ordered two units totalling eighty to a hundred men with red Swastika armbands and rifles to the scene where they started herding prisoners away from the houses and back onto the beach.

Later in the early the morning of the 3rd May the Volkssturm militiamen were reinforced by naval marines and the Gendarmes, SS and Gestapo guards under Hauptmann Otto Schmidt who had been resting up at the U-Boot-Schule. The stage was set for another massacre.

Fregattenkapitän Friedrich Ziemann was the commander of the marines on the beach that day. In the evidence he subsequently gave to the British investigators he admitted witnessing three prisoners shot for stealing from local German citizens, prisoners shot because they were too sick to leave the barges, and prisoners shot because they were unable to keep up on the march which took them from e Pelzerhaken into Neustadt.

Ziemann's account looks a masterpiece of understatement.

A Polish prisoner Władysław Binder said, "Those still aboard the barges were tossed overboard and killed. One elderly woman tried to make her way to a ladder on all fours; she was slowly going down the rungs into the water. The sailor fires three shots at her, and finally finished her off with a revolver."

The Germans in fact shot everyone who didn't swiftly wade ashore from the *Vaterland* and murdered every prisoner still aboard. One SS guard, identified by three Danish prisoners – Helge Larsen, Hans Christian Staub and Helge Kierulf –as Johannes Pettke, a violent

alcoholic, chose to use a hammer for the task rather his sub-machine gun.

As for the march into Neustadt, a Jewish prisoner, Jankel Leib Schneider gave evidence that, "We who were already standing at the shore, were lined up in groups and led to the U-Boot- Schule. During the march, those prisoners who could not keep up with the speed were either pushed into the sea and shot or executed right at the spot. In this way my friend Hari Pale who was walking next to me was shot because he could not walk any longer, and I had already no force to drag him along anymore."

Even some local citizens seem to have been appalled at the level of violence. Heinrich Marsen, who lived near the beach said, "I saw a prisoner who was weak being shot by navy personnel in front of my house. The shooting lasted in all from about 10.00 to 11.00 am. After the shooting and when the other prisoners had marched away, I saw about 100 bodies lying on the beach between my house and the Lotzenhaus. At the rear of the column of prisoners going in the direction of Neustadt were the navy personnel. Shortly after they moved off, I heard still more shots in the woods."

Reaching the sports field adjacent to the U-Boot-Schule may have brought an end to the shootings but not to the suffering of the survivors. Despite the proximity of a large hospital, they were denied medical attention and after receiving drinking water and soup, they were marched down to the harbour with the intention of embarkation onto one of the prison ships in the bay just in time to witness an RAF attack on the anchored fleet.

In 1947, Major Noel Till of the British No. 2 War Crimes Investigation Team produced a detailed report laying the principal responsibility for the Neustadt massacres on Gendarmerie-Hauptmann Otto Schmidt and Fregattenkapitän Heinrich Schmidt the city Kommandant. Later evidence also suggested that Kapitänleutnant Ziemann bore responsibility too since in briefing the marines that morning he falsely told them that the escapees were

subhumans who had already murdered German women and children and that he issued orders to shoot immediately any prisoner fleeing or resisting arrest.

No charges or war crimes trial ensued even when in 2015 the district attorney of Lübeck closed a lengthy investigation of events at Pelzerhaken on 3rd May 1945 and concluded that 77 prisoners were murdered in or near the barges on the beach, 10 who reached the next village of Merkendorf were shot dead there, and about 170 were shot after being rounded up while being marched from Pelzerhaken to the U-Boot-Schule in central Neustadt.

Stutthof to Nickelswalde: 27th April

The next evacuation from Stutthof took place on 27th April under the command of SS-Unterscharführer Herbert Karl Holst and it involved the last 3,000 remaining inmates. The only exceptions were to be a handful of prisoners involved with camp administration and about 1,000 people deemed too near death to travel.

The journey to Nickelswalde took the form of two marching columns and narrow-gauge railway transportation for those too sick to walk, many of whom were naked beneath ragged blankets because, as Max Mäder, a German prisoner working as a medical orderly at Stutthof testified, the 450 prisoners at the sick bay were provided with clothing for just 50 persons.

The first marching column headed up by SS-Oberscharführer Wagner arrived in good time to meet the planned departure time of 03.00. The timing was critical because the voyage to Hel needed to be completed in the hours of darkness to minimise the risk of attacks by Russian aircraft. The loading of prisoners was not without incident, however. The guards struck and used their whips to speed up the embarkation and prisoners falling into the water were shot. A Pole, Stefan Bodzanowski described what happened: "I saw two prisoners being pushed off the plank as their comrades were crowding after them and fall into the divide between the barge and

the bank. They tried to crawl ashore. Here Wanserski was standing firing his pistol at the two men who were still in the water."

Some twenty prisoners died in such incidents including those who received fatal injuries from being thrown by guards into the holds of the vessels which were to take them to Hel and beyond.

The second column of some 700 prisoners commanded by SS-Unterscharführer Wanserski was late – it did not arrive at Nickelswalde until 04.00 on the 28th. By then Wagner had already left on a naval landing craft, the F-862.

On the morning of 28th, Holst sent back to Stutthof for food. The resulting delivery of cauldrons of soup to Nickelswalde at 13.00 proved insufficient and the distribution ended chaotically with the strongest prisoners successfully fighting for whatever they could get. It was the same story with the butchering of a horse later that day which again resulted in many prisoners getting nothing at all.

By the evening of the 28th fifty desperately ill Jewish prisoners had been left lying unattended for many hours on the floors of the railway wagons in which they had been transported to Nickelswalde. The 21 German prisoners of the Umladekommando who had helped load the train at Stutthof were now ordered to remove them from the train to a nearby bomb crater. Then as Erich Nagel set down a Jewish woman unable to walk near where Unterscharführer Wanserski and SS-Sturmmann Wippermann were standing, Wanserski took out his pistol and shot her in the head.

Marian Smarzewski, a Polish prisoner, testified to what happened next. "The SS-men selected eight strong men from our group and gave them four blankets. Each blanket was carried by two prisoners. The SS-men led them to the train that was loaded with Jews and ordered them to carry those Jews who were not able to walk all the while the SS-men were aiding. The ill prisoners were carried out of the wagon, placed on the blankets, and carried to the excavation…The Jew in question was placed at the excavation; the SS sergeant threw a blanket on top of the Jew and shot him through

the blanket in the back of the head. Then he kicked the body into the excavation with his boot. He did that in front of our eyes."

Nickelswalde to Hel: Marinefährprahm F 862

Unlike the other vessels involved in the evacuation of Stutthof prisoners from Nickelswalde, the Marinefährprahm F862 was a fast, self-powered navy landing craft armed with anti-aircraft guns and a 7.5 cm cannon. It was however in a filthy state, not having been hosed down after its last cargo – a herd of live pigs.

In the early hours of 28th April 510 prisoners were loaded onto the vessel, 350 of them Jewish women and it departed - with a contingent exclusively made up of SS guards - as scheduled by the evacuation commander, SS-Oberscharführer Wagner, at 03.00. Wagner himself was on board.. He had left his deputy, SS-Unterscharführer Holst, to supervise the loading of the final vessel in the river, the barge *SB Ruth*.

The F-862 arrived at Hel at around 06.00 just in time to be caught up in an attack on the port by more than twenty Russian fighter-bombers. The captain executed a series of rapid manoeuvres to avoid falling bombs and Soviet machine guns and as a crew member, Signalmaat Ludwig Bresch later recollected, "We curved around at the roadstead like madmen: hard starboard, hard port, zigzag line, extreme speed ahead in order not to present the attacking aircraft with a target. During that, an old woman fell overboard… The old woman was on deck holding on to the railing as the alarm started. The anchor was up, and as we took off, the sudden movement made her fall overboard. Some people yelled: *Man overboard!* In any normal situation we would have made an effort to rescue her but with the attackers above our heads, the captain just sailed off and paid no attention to the woman."

There was no prospect of rescuing her nor any chance to carry out their orders which had been to disembark all the Typhus sufferers at Hel for re-embarkation on a larger vessel. Instead the landing craft headed West. Unfortunately, Swinemünde proved equally

inaccessible because it too was already under Russian assault with the German military preparing to blow up the port.

By 2nd May and flying a yellow quarantine flag in recognition of the number of Typhus cases aboard, the F-862 had skirted Lübeck and Neustadt, which were about to fall to the allies, and later that same day was attacked near Kiel by British warplanes, sustaining major damage. Many of the prisoners were killed as well as guards and some of the crew and the ship began to burn.

Rescue for some survivors arrived in response to the distress call made by the wounded captain of the F-862 in the shape of rope ladders thrown down by another ship which took off some crew members, most of the SS guards and the luckiest 150 of the prisoners. One of the inmates, Hanni Krispin explained just how fortunate she was. "From that ship, rope ladders were suddenly lowered. And sailors came and helped us….Then 150 people was taken unto that ship….But then they decided: they could take no more than 150, because the ship couldn't carry more….And we had the luck that all the food they had was oatmeal. And they poured the oatmeal in a small pot and gave every one of us a small portion, so that everyone gets something. And then they cooked more, and then more again, so that everyone of us got something to eat."

To starving people who had not eaten in days that must have seemed a miracle of sorts even if it was a not entirely altruistic gesture from the German seamen. As Frieda Ben David observed once aboard their resuer's ship "The crew asked: *Who are you, you look like a crowd…* When we replied: *We come from a concentration camp,* they wanted to know, what crime we had done. *Our only crime is being Jewish*, we said. Then they helped us a little and asked immediately: *Will you testify after the end of the war that we helped you?*"

Nor was the reception afforded to the survivors back on land overly welcoming. As the wounded and burnt were being disembarked in Kiel watched by local civilians, a man in uniform started throwing

crusts of bread at them, apparently hoping to provoke a fight among the desperate prisoners.

Back at sea, the F-862 was afire, taking on water and listing dangerously. There were still three SS-guards, some crew members the captain and up to fifty sick, wounded and badly burnt prisoners on board, although a number had flung themselves into the water to escape the flames and drowned. Presently the fires were extinguished and the vessel limped along the coast for several hours until the captain was able to beach it near Bookniseck in the Bay of Eckernförde where the SS guards went ashore and absconded.

Two local landowners are credited for saving prisoner lives on the following morning. Graf Oscar von Moltke-Kirsten and Friedrich Freiherr von Ahlefeldt had the survivors transported by tractor and trailer to find them food and medical treatment. Even so more died of exposure in the hours they spent on the open trailers and at the hospitals at Kappeln and Eckernförde some doctors refused to treat them because they were Jews even though by then they had been fed and bathed at a nearby naval facility and exchanged their rags for the uniforms of Luftwaffenhelferinnen - female air force auxiliaries. It was at von Moltke-Kirsten's insistence that they finally received the care they so desperately needed.

The death toll among the Stutthof inmates on the F-862 was staggeringly high; less than a third survived the ten-day voyage.

Nickelswalde to Hel: The Ruth

Carrying around 500 concentration camp evacuees into the German *Umladekommando* prisoners, seventeen SS guards and SS-Unterscharführer Kurt Wanserski's wife, mother-in-law and female friend – Wanserski was plainly decamping permanently to safer climes - the *SB Ruth* departed Nickelswalde under tow from a former icebreaker, the *S/T Pregel.* She was already flying a yellow quarantine flag because of the number of Typhus cases on board.

The barge moored briefly off Hel for Unterscharführer Wanserski to receive new orders at 03.00 morning of 29th April, two hours after leaving Nickelswalde but was not permitted to land any of its occupants and they soon set sail again as part of a small convoy of assorted vessels. Two torpedo boats from the convoy would end up escorting the barge and its tugboat to Flensburg on the Schleswig-Holstein coast.

Adolf Hitler committed suicide on 30th April in his bunker in the Reich Chancellory garden in Berlin and the city fell to the Soviets on 2nd May. Hitler's successor as Führer, Admiral Dönitz, had already set up his governmental headquarters at the Naval Academy at Mürwik near Flensburg. If Dönitz had cared to look out of his office window on the 3rd or 4th May he would have seen, moored at an otherwise deserted pier below, a filthy, dilapidated river barge full of sick and dying Stutthof evacuees. Forbidden entry to the port of Saßnitz on Rügen Island, they had drifted along the coast for two days before fetching up at Mürwik only because the latest embargo had prohibited their entry into the port of Flensburg.

A working party of prisoners left the *S/B Ruth* on the morning of 4th tasked with burying the bodies of thirty dead prisoners near the beach. Later that day Kapitan Paul Biefeldt received permission to enter the harbour of Flensburg but it was not until 5th that he was able to transfer most of his prisoners onto a larger cargo ship, the *S/S Rheinfels* already carrying evacuees from Neuengamme sub-camps and moored outside the harbour at the Flensburg roadstead. Biefeldt was also permitted to send about 130 very weak prisoners to the Malteser Krankenhaus St. Franziskus Catholic Hospital and the Evangelical-Lutheran Flensburg City Hospital

The problem for the 1,360 prisoners incarcerated on the *SS Rheinfels* in terrible conditions was that there was nowhere to go and no hope of any positive intervention until 10th when the Swedish Red Cross were finally permitted to take control of the vessel, transfer the prisoners onto a better ship, *M/S Homburg*, and supply them with

food and mattresses in preparation for the voyage across to Malmö in Sweden where they could be convalesced and rehabilitated.

Many of the prisoners still carried Typhus and there were more deaths to come and considerable danger to their Red Cross saviours. Some of them were infected and died too, like the nurse Gertrud Fröberg.

Surprisingly perhaps, the overall death toll on the *S/B Ruth* has been estimated at less than fifty people, mostly from disease and thirst, despite a reported incident of panic among prisoners demanding water as the vessel left Hel, in response to which an SS officer fired his pistol into the crowded cargo hold. Evidence as to the identity of the officer was conflicting. One prisoner, Karl Schwartz thought it was Unterscharführer Holst while another, Wilhelm Vosseler attributed it to Unterscharführer Wanserski: "When the prisoners shouted in the holds, he fired into the holds calling *If you're not quiet, I shall kill a lot of you.*"

At least one of the dead was murdered by a fellow prisoner because he had managed to keep some water hidden. Franz Basel saw the body on 1st May of a "Jew has 26 knife wounds in his back for one bottle of water, knife taken away and hidden."

Although the death toll was vastly worse on the other vessels which left Nickelswalde in late April 1945, the limited British capacity to investigate such war crimes led to a focus on the massacre of fifty Jews at Nickelswalde as the *S/B Ruth* was being loaded and the treatment of the embarkees who were largely deprived of even water for the six days of the voyage - such water as there was had been distributed only to the guards and a few select prisoners - during that barge's voyage. The findings of Major Noel Till of the War Crimes No.2 Investigation Unit resulted in the only war crimes trial relating to the marine evacuation of Stutthof prisoners *(see Part 9 below)*.

The last, seemingly unnecessary, tragedy to befall Stutthof evacuees happened to those who had survived the January death marches to end up imprisoned ona huge ship moored in the bay, the *S/S Cap Arcona.*

Built by Blohm & Voss in Hamburg in 1927, the *Cap Arcona*, a moderately well appointed ocean liner, bore some resemblance to the *R/M/S Titanic* in the eyes of the German film director, Herbert Selpin. She was not as large as the Titanic and had only three funnels instead of four. However, on film she could pass muster as the tragic vessel striking an iceberg so in 1942, at Selpin's insistence, she was commandeered from training and troopship duties by order of Josef Goebbels to star in a the propaganda film. The plot of the film had British greed and capitalism responsible for a tragedy lessened only by the heroism of a fictional first officer of German origin. The film did not sink without trace but was withdrawn soon after its release in 1943 because the drownings of most of the cast proved too close a reminder to the grim sacrifices of a war the Germans were beginning to look like losing. It was an ill omen indeed.

The *Cap Arcona* was eventually handed back to the Kreigsmarine and on 31st January 1945 was used to evacuate German troops and civilians from East Prussia despite the increasing risk posed by mines and Soviet submarines. Her next trip on 30th March was to be equally perilous - fetching troops and refugees from Gotenhafen (Gydnia) and rather than face leaving Copenhagen, the captain, Johannes Gertz, shot himself. His ship survived the voyage anyway but her turbines were now past effective repair and she was moored up to perform her final service as a prison ship under the command of Heinrich Bertram, accommodating concentration camp inmates evacuated from Neuengamme as the camps were cleared to prevent the enormity of the horrors perpetrated there being discovered by the advancing allies. Many of those prisoners had previously been at Stutthof.

On 2nd May 1945 barges carried their final load of some 800 more prisoners out into the Bay of Lübeck. The *S/S Cap Arcona* already had over 5,000 prisoners on board and little in the way of food or medical supplies and so refused to accept any more. In any event since the vessel and another prison ship, the *Thielbek*, were unseaworthy, even if they had been accepted on board this final load of prisoners would not have been carried to freedom in neutral Sweden as was subsequently falsely claimed by Gauleiter Karl Kaufmann. He was in fact merely attempting to cleanse Hamburg of human evidence of atrocities before arranging its surrender to advancing British and Canadian troops. It was a fairly pointless attempt since the allies had already taken Neuengamme on 2nd May capturing whatever evidence of remained and Major-General Philip Roberts had been informed by the International Red Cross that at least 7,000 prisoners were being held aboard ships in the Bay of Lübeck.

By that afternoon a British reconnaissance unit was advancing along the coast to discover ships burning in the bay but they were able only to rescue a few severely emaciated victims on the beach at Neustadt among the bodies of massacred women and children. They were too late to prevent the sinkings that followed.

The former ocean liner carried no Red Cross insignia or any other visible sign of its cargo. Indeed it was never intended to survive its last purpose. Hamburg's Police chief, Georg-Henning Graf von Bassewitz-Behr, would later testify that the prisoners on the ship were to be killed to comply with Himmler's orders that no trace of the concentration camps should remain for the allies to find. Another officer, Kurt Rickert, testified at the Hamburg War Crimes Trial that the ships were to be sunk by the Luftwaffe or U-boats and Eva Neurath from Neustadt stated she had been told by a police officer that the ships held convicts and were going to be blown up. However the RAF saved the Germans the task.

The vital information that the *Cap Arcona*, the *Deutschland* and the *Thielbek* were carrying concentration camp prisoners never reached the Hawker Typhoon pilots of Squadron Nos. 184, 193, 197, 198 and 263 who were deployed to harass and sink shipping along the Baltic coast. Indeed the RAF believed the ships had been gathered to carry fleeing SS personnel to a neutral country and attacked them accordingly.

Severely damaged and set ablaze by rocket fire, the *Cap Arcona* eventually capsized taking down with it most of the unfortunate prisoners. Those who made it into the water then had to endure strafing by RAF cannon fire. Only about 350 were rescued by German trawlers along with 16 sailors, 400 SS guards, and 20 *Aufseherinnen.* The reason most of the guards survived was simply because they had life jackets and the former concentration camp inmates did not. Similarly all but 50 of the 2,800 inmates on the *Thielbek* died. Those on the *Deutschland* fared better - all 2,000 prisoners were rescued before the ship went down.

For weeks afterwards the bodies of those who had, until then, survived Stutthof and Neuengamme kept washing up on the shore, to be buried in mass graves.

Back at Stutthof, the camp was the target during March and April 1945 of several Soviet air attacks and a bomb hit the Jewish hospital on March 26th, killing twenty-eight and wounding another thirty-five. After that air and artillery strikes became more frequent. As a former Jewish inmate later recalled; "The Stutthof camp was enormous and from one end to the other it was burning down from the air attacks. Countless numbers of Katzetler [inmates] were killed by the bombs. I myself was lucky, because a bomb hit our ward and three-quarters of the sick were killed or wounded."

Eventually the last remaining SS-guards started the final liquidation of the camp by burning down the Jewish barracks even though sick

prisoners were still inside. It was the last SS act of murder after which they fled, rather than risk capture by the Russians.

Soviet forces in the shape of soldiers of the 48th Army under the command of Colonel Cyplenkow finally liberated Stutthof on May 9th 1945, rescuing about 100 prisoners who had managed to hide during the final SS liquidation.

As with the main camp, Stutthof's subsidiary camps had been largely emptied by the SS before the Red Army arrival and the inmates were divided into those deemed fit enough to be force marched westwards and those selected for immediate death. At Elbing the killing was the made the responsibility of a Hungarian medic who chose to administer diluted or reduced dosages of the deadly injection, presumably of Phenol. If the victims feigned death they had at least a chance of survival and several were still alive when the Soviets arrived. Among them were four Lithuainian Jewesses, Chaja Verblunsky, her friend Riva Rubin and each of their mothers.

Tragically first Riva and then her mother died within the next month while being held in an abandoned school under Russian control. Chaja, whose however, lived through three years in displaced persons camps in Poland and Austria before emigrating to Canada to marry and start a new life as Helen Yermis.

Stutthof was back in use by October 1945 as a Prisoner of War camp. Nor was the suffering of former Stutthof inmates necessarily over and many in Red Army occupied territory were to disappear into the Soviet gulags. Others, particularly the women, were directly abused by their supposed liberators and the post-war Polish authorities had to establish a specialist hospital unit near Poznán and Thorún to treat sexually transmitted diseases contracted during rapes committed by Russian soldiers.

Even those who thought they might return to their home towns could find reintegration impossible for no fault of their own. Thus, Alexander Lebenstein, born in 1927, a German Jew abandoned at Stutthof in the last days due to his bad health fled to Frankfurt to

avoid having to join the Red Army, was turned away by the Americans who viewed him as a Russian responsibility, journeyed to his home town, Haltem am See, only to have his German citizenship denied and ended up in a Displaced Persons camp at Deggendorf in Bavaria after which was finally able to join a sister who had settled in America in 1939.

There would be no quick and simple return to normality for so many of the poor souls like Lebenstein who had lost so much but whom the SS had failed to kill between 1939 and 1945 in Stutthof.

Nevertheless the war was over. Justice and retribution were still to come. For most neither ever arrived.

The abandoned Stutthof camp

Watchtower and barbed wire at Stutthof

Death march into Germany 1945

The Cap Arcona

Barge evacuees from Stutthof 1945

River barges used in the evacuation of former Stutthof inmates

Danish Stutthof survivors returning to Copenhagen in June 1945 National Museum Of Denmark

The camp abandoned

PART 9
AFTERMATH

DIFFICULTIES arise in relation to interpreting certain aspects of the history of Stutthof for several reasons.

The first issue is that the Russian liberators of the camp in preparing investigatory reports for future war crimes trials had a strong motive for making their findings as black as possible – Stalin's gulags were to appear benign in comparison to the activities of Hitler's SS. Conversely the British and American investigations were fairly perfunctory, the fundamental imperative being the high profile trial at Nuremberg of the principal Nazis they had captured.

The second and most fundamental issue is that the brutalised survivors of the camp were not necessarily eye witnesses to mass executions or specific murders by sadistic guards but gained their awareness that such things were happening from the grapevine within Stutthof and its sub-camps. Accordingly, what they believed might well be true but incapable of being evidenced to the extent a normal criminal trial would require or sadly their recollections might have been twisted in the re-telling.

The third issue is the dissemination of matters deemed to be facts by third parties even after they have been disproved which has only provided ammunition for holocaust deniers.

It cannot be stressed enough that tens of thousands died because of their incarceration at Stutthof and all inmates were subject to an inhumanly repressive regime which cared not at all whether they lived or died. The problem is just that the reported death toll at Stutthof is difficult to substantiate or to refute.

According to the Russians up to 85,000 inmates of Stutthof died and in criminal proceedings brought in a German court at Muenster as recently as November 2018, the figure of 65,000 deaths was quoted as fact even though a death toll of that level from an inmate population of some 110,000 prisoners would substantially exceed the death ratios of camps liberated by the British and Americans, such as the infamous Bergen-Belsen at which the accepted death toll is 30,000.

The main reason for the discrepancy between such figures and the circa 26,800 sequentially numbered death certificates issued daily by SS administrators is said to be the non-inclusion of persons executed on immediate arrival at Stutthof by direct order from Berlin. That could certainly account for some significant discrepancy – if such prisoners were never inducted into the camp and registered, their murders would not attract the official registration of death normally required for SS record-keeping, especially if the execution orders from Berlin were among the records which were destroyed. However a difference of tens of thousands is a lot of unproven deaths for a camp which had only a small gas chamber, no obvious means of carrying out large scale executions other than by shooting and a long history of inability to dispose of corpses in times of cholera or other disease outbreaks outbreak through the camp's cremation ovens.

The original Russian figures from 1945 relied upon the estimated use of Stutthof's gas chamber to kill up to 150 people a time and cremation of up to 12 emaciated bodies in each oven per hour giving a disposal capacity of 288 inmates a day. These estimates are unsustainable. Eyewitnesses after the war talked of 75-100 Jewish women being crammed into the gas chamber while Professor Marek Orski of Gdańsk University estimated the gas chamber capacity to be as low as 25-30 adults. He has also asserted that trying to cremate more than two or three bodies at a time in an oven would block the air intakes and slow cremation to a point where the contents would take many hours to burn. In any event emaciated corpses with minimal fat burn poorly and incompletely.

Taking all these factors into account it seems that the true death toll for Stutthof as a concentration camp might have been something like half that claimed in 1945.

However, to such a figure can then be added the substantial death toll occurring on evacuation of the camp which is estimated to have caused 16,000-25,000 deaths and could substantiate a final tally of up to 65,00 deaths of people originally imprisoned at Stutthof.

Whatever the truth is, finding it has been considerably assisted by the Stutthof Museum's creation of a database from its files on 81,295 of the estimated 110,000 inmates of the camp. The amount of information contained in each file varies but ultimately the museum hopes to create a personal record for all prisoners held at the camp.

The overall death toll is far from being the only issue to which rumour and suspicion applied. The assertion has been repeatedly made that because of the small gas chamber capacity at Stutthof, a converted railway wagon was used. Thus Paweł Krupiński has stated as fact that "The killing of female prisoners in railway cars took place in…Stutthof…as part of *Operation Sonderbehandlung*…It is estimated that about 2,000 people died." Krupiński quotes directly from the memoirs of the prisoner, Aldo Coradello. "Under the guise of working in an external camp to repair stockings, darning socks, etc. groups of women were selected and then given needles and threads. Suspecting nothing, they boarded the narrow-gauge railway cars. Then, the train departed and, after passing one or two stations, returned to the camp. On departure, Zyklon B granules were thrown into the sealed wagon. The corpses were unloaded from the returning transport and burned in the crematorium."

There is certainly evidence from other camps of vehicular conversion into mobile gas chambers and it cannot be ruled out that this happened at Stutthof. The difficulty posed for historians is that there appears to be no surviving evidence that such converted railway trucks existed. If they did then they could only have been used in the immediate vicinity of Stutthof because of the region's unique narrow-gauge railway lines and some trace of its existence should have been found within a fairly tight geographical area. Thus the story may be true but cannot now be further unsubstantiated. In any event Stutthof was not one of the camps named in the implementation orders for Aktion 14f13, *Operation Sonderbehandlung* (special treatment) under which ill or non-productive workers fell to be exterminated.

Another more pervasive myth is that Jewish corpses were rendered down into soap and that story can still be found on multiple websites to this day. It's rare to be able to track such a belief to an actual source but the fragmentary truth from which the human soap story arose can be traced back to Stutthof which supplied a small number of corpses to Danzig's Anatomical Research Institute for making laboratory skeletons for teaching purposes. Other camps and prisons did the same and indeed this appears to have been the fate of the body of Captain Antoni Kasztelan which was passed to the Anatomy Institute of of the University of Konigsberg.

The Danzig institute headed by the pathologist Rudolph Spanner used giant macerating drums to cleanse the skeletons they received of flesh and it was noted that a fatty by-product of the process gathered on the surface which Spanner went on to use in articulating the joints of the skeletons. Apparently set to work within the institute were some British prisoners of war and it was either they or Aleksy Opiński, a laboratory worker at the Institute who started to spread the macabre story that the Germans were turning Jewish bodies into soap. The rumour of soap production from corpses was investigated after the war and discovered to be unfounded and Dr Spanner was never charged with any criminal offence. This did not stop Zofia Nałkowska naming Spanner and the Danzig Anatomical Institute in her collection of war atrocity stories entitled *Medallions* which was published in 1947 and fuelled by her writing it remains to this day an object of faith in some quarters that Jews were turned into soap by the Nazis on an industrial scale.

The Moscow Declaration of 1943 had settled the approach the Allied Powers, America, Britain, France and Russia, would take on handling war crime investigation and trials. A military-style tribunal would be convened to try the major Nazi war criminals, meaning those responsible for the strategies and decisions leading to the commencement and waging of war with scant regard for international standards governing the conduct of warfare (such as the treatment of civilians and of prisoners of war) and for the policies and

implementation of wholesale religious and ethnic extermination as well as for the other policies which shaped the operation of the concentration camps. The tribunal would comprise American, British and Russian judges. Poland, Czechoslovakia, France, Holland and other occupied countries would not be represented at these prosecutions.

It was also agreed that the cases of individual officers and men responsible for specific atrocities would be remitted for trial in and by the countries where their crimes had taken place.

Accordingly, none of the major Nazis connected to Stutthof would be tried at the main Nuremberg Tribunals because their crimes took place exclusively in Poland and they fell to be extradited and tried there if anywhere. Conversely if an individual the Polish authorities might wish to try had committed serious offences against allied troops or on German soil then they would be unlikely to get the opportunity to place them on trial before a Polish court.

On May 24th, the Polish government in exile in London issued a list of individual Nazis they would wish to see indicted for war crimes. Foremost on that list were the names of Arthur Greiser and Albert Forster.

Greiser left Posnan on 20th January 1945 having issued a general evacuation order for the city. He surrendered to the American army in Austria and was extradited to Poland where he was tried the following year becoming in the process the first person to be convicted of a new crime established by the victorious allies - *Waging aggressive war.*

Greiser's defence that he was only obeying orders was given short shrift when the prosecutors showed that other Gauleiters had not acted in exactly the same way as Greiser had. He was found guilty of all charges and sentenced to death and confiscation of all his property.

In the early morning of 21st July 1946 he was transported from prison to the slope of Fort Winary where he was hanged in front of a large crowd of onlookers, the last public execution to take place in Poland.

Albert Forster was not among the 10,000 surrendering combatants or the estimated 39,000 dead defenders of his city when Danzig fell to the Russians on 30th March 1945. He had shipped himself and his senior officers out on a special train to the port at Hel. The train served for a short while as both his headquarters and his billet but he was soon evacuated by submarine. He travelled only as far as Hamburg where he was captured on 27th May 1945 and interned at the British-administered Lager Fallingbostel. His true identity and record were only discovered fourteen months later at which point he was transferred to another internment camp at Neuengamme and then extradited to Poland on 10th October 1946.

Forster was charged with mass murder, tried by the Polish National Supreme Court at Gdańsk between April 4th and 29th 1948 and sentenced to death.

In June 1951 he was turned over to the Polish security service and subsequently there was recurring speculation that the death sentence had been commuted to life imprisonment. The official story is that Forster was hanged on 28th February 1952 at Warsaw's Mokotow Prison after an appeal for clemency to the Polish President was refused.

The next important names for those seeking justice for crimes committed at Stutthof were the the camp's two Kommandants.

Max Pauly was never tried on any charge relating to Stutthof. Instead he was put on trial in Hamburg by the British between 18th March and 13th May 1946 for multiple atrocities which occurred at Neuegamme under his command. These included the twenty Jewish children of Polish, Dutch and Czech origin brought specifically from Auschwitz for medical experiments by Kurt Heissmeyer into tuberculosis drug development.

In April 1945 in fulfilment of standing orders to prevent evidence of the purpose and management of concentration camps falling into allied hands, Pauly had the children transported to the basement of the Bullenhuser Damm School in Hamburg where they were rendered unconscious with morphine and hanged. The other potential witnesses, their nurses, were executed at the same time but without the mercy of opiate-induced unconsciousness.

Found guilty and sentenced to death with 11 other defendants Pauly was hanged by the executioner Albert Pierrepoint in Hamelin Prison on 8th October 1946.

The second Kommandant of Stutthof, Paul-Werner Hoppe, was captured by the British in April 1946 in Holstein but escape led to a long delay in bringing him to trial.

In the event he was sentenced to to only five years imprisonment which was later extended to nine years.

One significant man who did not survive to be tried was Stutthof's chief doctor from 1942-1945, Dr. Otto Heidl. Arrested and held in Bochum in 1955 pending investigation, Dr. Heidl hanged himself in custody.

When it came to the lower ranked SS guards who had served at Stutthof, several trials took place but all together these brought to justice only seventy-two SS officers and six female staff from Stutthof out of over 2,000 employed at the camp during its six-year existence. An appendix at the end of this book gives the names and sentence details but one unusual element is very clear; although the overwhelming majority of guards were men, a disproportionate number of women were put on trial and even amongst those tried the women were more likely to receive a death sentence.

The proportion of men and women captured and tried for crimes at Stutthof is not apparently reflective of the situation across Germany where female guards melted back into the population and were less

readily identifiable than male SS personnel unencumbered as they were by any mandatory blood group tattoos.

It was different for female guards in and around Danzig who were often locally recruited from families in the Danzig area which left them more vulnerable to discovery and capture.

Given the greater enthusiasm brought by the Russians and the Poles to war crimes trials, there may also be an element in the sentences meted out that considered similarly brutal behaviour as more reprehensible if carried out by female guards than males.

The first trial was held between April 25 and May 3 1946. Arraigned were thirty ex-officials and prisoner-guards of the camp; all were found guilty and eleven defendants were sentenced to death; the rest being sentenced to various terms of imprisonment.

The second trial was held from January 8 to 31 1947. Arraigned were twenty-four ex-officials and guards of the Stutthof concentration camp; all were found guilty and ten were sentenced to death.

The third trial was held from November 5 to 10 1947. Arraigned were twenty ex-officials and guards; nineteen were found guilty and one was acquitted.

The fourth and final mass trial was held, from November 19 to 29 1947. Arraigned were twenty-seven ex-officials and guards; twenty-six were found guilty and one was acquitted.

A fifth trial was held in Torun in 1949 and a last Stutthof trial in Poland took place in 1953 in Gdańsk but these were single defendant cases with each receiving a term of imprisonment.

Away from Poland, on 25th September 25 1946, a British Military Tribunal convened in Flensburg to try twelve defendants for the barbaric treatment of Stutthof evacuees both at Nickelswalde, where fifty Jews were shot while awaiting embarkation, and during the voyage to Flensburg on the *S/B Ruth*. Strangely, the evacuation

commander, Unterscharführer Kurt Wanserski, was not on trial although his deputy, Unterscharführer Herbert Karl Holst, was.

On 23rd October 1946, the tribunal pronounced judgment, sentencing Holst, SS-Sturmmann Herbert Walbrecht and SS-Sturmmann Otto Wilhelm Wippermann to death. The sentences were not subsequently commuted and the executions were carried out. Another police functionary, Ernst Bouvier, was sentenced to two years imprisonment for ill-treatment of embarking prisoners and the other eight accused were acquitted.

A much more recent development has arisen because of a change in the law and prosecution policy in Germany which has effectively removed any time limitation on trying war crimes. This has led to a handful of recent cases, among them the trial which commenced in the Muenster State Court on November 6th 2018 of the ninety-four-year old Johann Rehbogen as an accessory to hundreds of murders by virtue of his position as a guard at Stutthof from June 1942 to September 1944.

Specific charges in Rehbogen's case related to the deaths of over 100 Polish prisoners gassed in June 1944 and subsequent gassings of Jewish prisoners between August and December 1944. In a statement read by his lawyer, the defendant acknowledged that he was aware of the mass cremation of corpses but maintained that he did not know about wholesale killings or the operation of the camp's gas chamber. The trial was subsequently ended following hospitalisation with heart and kidney problems deemed to render him permanently unfit to stand trial.

A second Stutthof guard, Bruno Dey, was charged in Hamburg in 2019 as an accessory to 5,230 murders at the camp. Dey's testimony is important because he reportedly admitted hearing screams coming from the camp's gas chamber and he is thus a first-hand eye witness to murder by Zyklon B gas, something alleged to have happened repeatedly at Stutthof as elsewhere.

Dey's background is instructive. Training to be a baker must have seemed to him a safe trade with prospects. Learning skills which would remain essential when peace finally arrived meant he largely evaded the war's worst excesses. Unfortunatly his luck changed suddenly in the summer of 1944 when the Ministry of Labour drafted the young man and on August 9th shipped him to Stutthof to serve as a concentration camp guard. He was seventeen.

At this remove nobody knows in any detail what duties Bruno Dey performed at Stutthof while serving there for nine months until April 26th 1945. However, in 2019, some seventy-four years later, it would be enough that Dey was there as a watchtower guard from August 1944 to April 1945, an SS private among the two thousand men and women who enabled the Stutthof Concentration Camp to function. He was identified from a photograph by the Stutthof survivor Judy Meisel as the man they called *Meydele* in Yiddish – meaning *young girl* - because of his absurdly juvenile features.

Undoubtedly Dey carries moral guilt for his role as a small cog in a murderous machine but at this remove, in default of first-hand evidence, legal guilt for specific acts of murder would seem impossible to establish beyond reasonable doubt. But then again, applying the words of the Nazi-hunter Simon Weisenthal, *there's nobody alive who's qualified to forgive him either*. The solution as German prosecutors eventually decided has been to charge defendants like Bruno Dey as accessories whose roles aided and abetted murder making them complicit in the crimes against humanity that took place in concentration camps. Dey was convicted by a court in Hamburg in July 2020 and given a two year suspended sentence due to his age – he was 93 at the date he was convicted and wheelchair-bound.

The latest case to come before the German courts in 2021 concerned Irmgard Furchner, born in Danzig in 1925 who as Irmgard Dirksen worked at Stutthof between 1943 and 1945 as a typist and secretary to the Kommandant Paul Werner-Hoppe. Her duties including the transcription of execution orders in an office overlooking the main

camp making it implausible that she did not know what was happening there. On 20th December 2022 Furchner received a suspended sentenced of two years imprisonment

The Stutthof survivor Manfred Goldberg said of the sentence, "It's a foregone conclusion that a 97-year-old would not be made to serve a sentence in prison – so it could only be a symbolic sentence but the length should be made to reflect the extraordinary barbarity of being found to be complicit in the murder of more than 10,000 people." He was of course right although no sentence imposed could, at this late a remove from the events of 1939-1945, truly reflect actual guilt.

Further such trials must shortly cease. Any defendant would at this point be in their late nineties and would have served at Stutthof as teenagers and then only in the last few months of the war. Death as the great leveller will have already claimed the overwhelming majority of Stutthof's SS guards and civilian employees.

In total about 170,000 investigations have taken place since 1945 in relation to concentration camps resulting in around 6,700 prosecutions. Astonishingly only 50 of these related to the 6,500 SS and civilians who served at Auschwitz.

By comparison, the extent of justice meted out on behalf of the victims of Stutthof, however inadequate, has covered a somewhat higher proportion of the 2,000 serving at Stutthof between 1939 and 1945, probably because the original prosecutions were in the hands of the Russians and Poles. Even so the overwhelming majority of those at Stutthof were never required to pay for their crimes not least because until the early years of the twenty-first century, it was German prosecution policy was to ignore so-called lower level offenders.

After the war, Stutthof itself did not remain empty. It was pressed into service by the Red Army and indeed some prisoners such as the Lithuanian playwright Balys Sruoga continued to be detained there for a short period before being allowed to return to Vilnius.

Ultimately when it was once again abandoned, the camp was raided by local people desperate for building materials to repair their own homes or to build new ones. If the wood and stones of those houses could speak, they might fill in some of the many remaining gaps in the history of Stutthof KL.

As it is the site now houses an excellent museum and the Death Gate, the core barrack rooms, fences, and watchtowers of the Old Camp have been preserved along with the brick-built Kommandantur and the Kommandant's villa. The museum also conserves a significant archive despite the incineration of key documents by the Germans at the time of the camp's evacuation. The Stutthof archives include personal details of about 85,000 former prisoners and much of the surviving documentation which was packed and transported with the evacuees and later found abandoned in the Spring of 1945 in a roadside ditch by the Red Army.

Inevitably there remain many unanswered questions about Stutthof and the inmates and their guards whose stories are touched upon in this book.

And finally there is the fate of the young boys pictured so graphically playing war games in the grounds of Stutthof of whom little is known beyond the bare fact that the war made them orphans. They had lived in the Kommandant's villa at Stutthof with their parents until 1942 when they moved into living quarters at Neuengamme KL as a consequence of their father's posting there. Then in August 1944 their mother died by which time they had three siblings.

In May 1945 the five children fled with their father but they didn't go far. They joined Max Pauly's sister-in-law in Wesselburen, his birthplace, and it was there that the allies found and arrested Pauly that autumn. After that the children's trail goes cold so it may never be known how the Pauly family dealt with the burden of guilt by association that must have come once the extent of their father's crimes became known and the basis for his trial and execution

understood. It's not even known if they kept his surname; if they were brought up by their aunt they may even have taken her surname.

In 1954, Pauly's body was moved from the grounds of Hamelin Prison into the nearby Am Wehl Cemetery which is now a park with trees and winding paths. The irony is that there must be at least a possibility that Pauly's children and grandchildren have walked and played there just as Stutthof was merely a playground for his two eldest sons..

Top left: Rudolph Spanner
Top right Jenny-Wanda Barkmann
Bottom: The abandoned gas chamber

Collecting evidence under Russian supervision 1945

Clockwise from top left: 1.Oswald Pohl 2.Max Pauly 3. Herte Botha

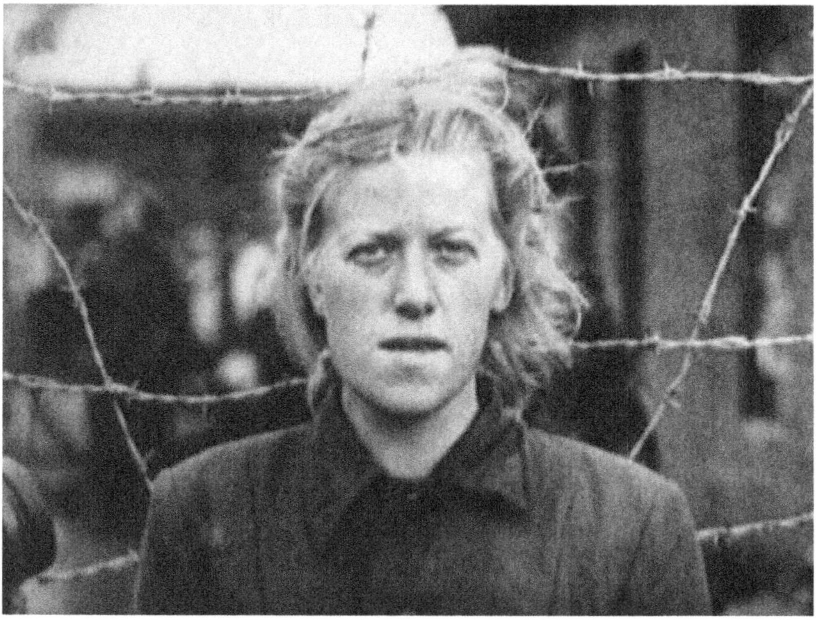

Left: Kurt Mathesius Right: Teodor Meyer

Dr. Otto Heidl

Albert Forster in captivity

At Stutthof with Polish guards during 1st Gdańsk Trial
1st row left to right Ewa Paradies, Elisabeth Becker & Wanda Klaff
2nd row Gerda Steinhoff, Jenny Barkmann

Top Left to right:
Hans Rach, Fritz Peters, Albert Paulitz, Ewald Foth, Theodor Meyer
Bottom Left to right
Elisabeth Becker, Erna Beilhardt, Gerda Steinhoff, Jenny-Barkmann, Wanda Klaff

Wanda Klaff's execution

Stutthof prisoner graffiti

Executions 4th July 1946
Top L-R: Barkman, Paradies, Becker, Klaff, Steinhoff
Bottom L-R: Steinhoff, Pauls

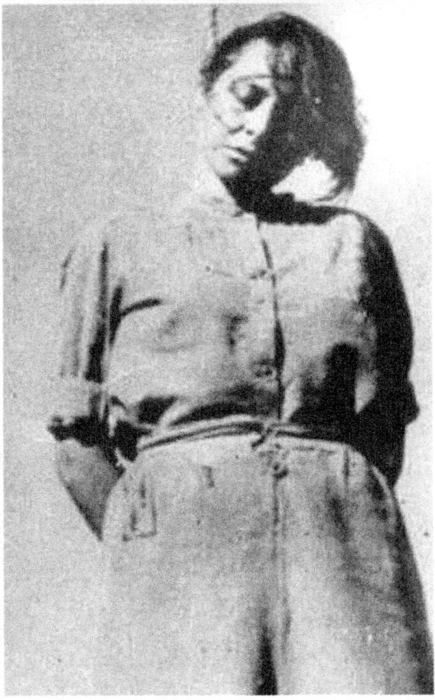

Trucks positioned for executions 4th July 1946
Left; Ewa Paradies Right: Jenny-Wanda Barkmann

APPENDIX I
KNOWN STUTTHOF SS GUARDS

Kommandants
HOPPE Paul Werner - *9 years imprisonment*
PAULY, Max – *hanged*
Senior Staff
BONIN Engelbrecht von
CHRISTOFFEL, Franz - *unknown sentence*
DITTMAN, Alfred
DRIEMEL, Alfred
EHLE, Paul - *died 1965*
GUST, Erich Gust (AKA GIESE, Franz)
MATHESIUS, Kurt
MEYER, Teodor – *hanged*
REDDIG, Richard
SCHWARTZ, Albert
SETTE, Ernst
VOGLER, Wilhelm
Adjutants
MULLER, Erich
STAHL, Josef
UNGER, Walter
Lagerarzt (SS Doctors)
HEIDL, Otto - *committed suicide*
JOBST, Willy – *executed*
OTTO, Johannes
VON SCHENK, Werner
WEDEL, Ernst *(dentist)*
Other Guards & Kapos
ADRIAN, Paul
AKOLT, Richard - *3 years imprisonment*
ALBRECHT, Johannes
ALLAUT, Andreas
ANKER, Paul
ARNOLD, Otto
BANSEMER, Rudolf
BASE, Paul
BAUMANN, Herbert
BAUMGARTNER, Leopold - *less than 1 year imprisonment*
BECK, Willi
BECKER, Heinrich
BECKER, Hermann
BEHNKE, Helmut
BIERNATH, Johann
BERG, Rudolf - *10 years imprisonment*
BLUMENAU, Willi
BÖHM, Ernst
BÖHM, Karl
BOLHAGEN, Kurt
BREIT, Jan – *hanged*
BRODOWSKI, Gustav - *less than 1 year imprisonment*
BUBLITZ, Alfred
BUNTROCK, Karl
BÜRGER, Richard Emil
BURNELEIT, Willy
BUTH, Willi - *life in prison*
CHILL, William
CZAJKOWSKI, Alfons
DAU, Hans
DEY, Bruno – *on trial 2019*
DIETERT, Hans
DIETRICH, Kurt – *executed*
DIRKS, Walter
DIRNBERGER, Nikolaus - *4 years imprisonment*

DOBERT, August
DOERKS, Eberhard
DREHER, Walter
EBERLE, Gustav - *10 years imprisonment*
ECKERMANN, Bernard - *less than 1 year imprisonment*
EGGERT, Karl – *executed*
EHLING, Hermann
EICHLER, Andreas
EICHLER, August
ELSDORFF, Herbert
ELTERMANN. Johann
ENGLER, Fritz
ENGLER, Herbert
ENGLERT, Walter - *3 years imprisonment*
ENSS, Heinrich
FALK, Felix
FAST, Wilhelm
FIGUR, Walter
FOTH, Ewald – *hanged*
FOTH, Ewald Paul
FRIEDLAND, Ernst
FULLE, Hubert
GALLANDT, Walter
GISELLA, Josef
GLASS, Alfons
GLAWE, Fritz - *10 years imprisonment*
GOERTZ, Johannes - *8 years imprisonment*
GOERKE, Paul
GÖHRT, Ewald
GÖIKE, Otto
GÖRSCH, Martin
GÖRTZ, Heinz
GÖRTZ, Johannes
GOTTSCHAU, Oskar - *10 years imprisonment*
GRÄBER, Kurt
GRABOWSKI, Paul
GRAMS, Adolf - *10 years imprisonment*
GRONING, Bruno
GROSS, Fritz
GRÜN, Max
HANDTKE, Kurt
HANNEMAN, Edwin
HANNEMAN, Ernst
HAPPKE, Eeich
HASS, Anton
HAUPT, Otto - *12 years imprisonment*
HEIN, Albert
HELD, Friedrich
HENKE, Waldemar - 5 years imprisonment
HERRMAN, Friedrich
HINTZ, Paul
HINTZ, Werner
HIRSBRUNNER, Otto
HÖLDTKE, Albert
HÖLDTKE, Willem
HOLZ, Herbert
HORZIG, Franz
ICHNOWSKI, Eugen
JÄGER, Helmut
JAHRSEN, Paul
JAKOBI, Hans
JAKUSCH, Bruno
JANZEN, August
JANZEN, Kurt
JASSEN, Erich - *10 years imprisonment*
JURTZICK, Hans
KAMIN, Paul
KARNATH, Walter
KAUTZ, Gustav - *5 years imprisonment*
KEWITSCH, Hans
KLAFFKE, Adolf - *10 years imprisonment*
KLAWAN, Nikolai - *3 years imprisonment*

KLEIN, Erwin
KLEIN, Prosper
KLEISS, Hermann
KLINGENBERG, Franz
KNABE, Helmut
KNEPPERT, Ernst - *less than 1 year imprisonment*
KNIFFKE, Anton - *3 years imprisonment*
KNOF, Alfred
KNOTT, Otto - *3 years imprisonment*
KNOTT, Willi
KOEPKE, Horst - *10 years imprisonment*
KOHBIETER, Walter
KÖNIG, Ernst
KÖPKE, Horst
KÖRBER, Albert
KOSSLER, Johann
KREFT, Siegfried
KRÖNKE, Erich
KROPP, Alfred
KROPP, Helmut
KRUGER or KRUEGER, Max
KRUMMEREICH, Bruno
KUHLMANN, Johannes
KUNATH, Edmund
KUNKEL, Paul
KUSCH, Artur
KUSCHEL, Erich
KUSCHEL, Rudolf
KUTNER, Johannes
LANGE, Ernst
LANGE, Richard
LASCHEIT, Emil - *10 years imprisonment*
LASNER, Robert
LAU, Paul
LEHNAU, Max
LEHNHOFF, Paul
LEISING, Josef
LEMKE, Erich
LESSAT, Alfred
LEWENDEL, Jakob
LICHTNER, Johann - *5 years imprisonment*
LIESKE, Johann
LIKERSKI, Franz
LINK, Hermann - *5 years imprisonment*
LOEWEN, Heinz - *5 years imprisonment*
LUEDTKE, Bernhard - *6 years imprisonment*
LÜDTKE, Rudolf
LUTZ, Hans
MAHLEE, Gustav
MAKOWSKI, Willi
MANKOWSKI, Hugo
MARZAN, Friedrich
MEIER, Anton
MEIER, Fritz
MEINCK, Karl Heinrich - *12 years imprisonment*
MEINHARDT, Gerhard
MEINHARDT, Paul
MEISSEL, Erich
MERTENS, Erich - *5 years imprisonment*
MERTINS, Fritz
MICHELSEN, Max
MIELENZ, Franz - *acquitted due to illness*
MIELENZ, Johannes
MIELKE, Erich
MOEHRKE, Hans - *4 years imprisonment*
MOLKENTHIN, Artur
MÖWE, Johann
MÖWE, Karl
MUELLER, Harry - *4 years imprisonment*
MÜLLER, Bernhard
MÜLLER, Leonhard

MURNER, Robert
NEUBAUER, Otto
NEUBAUER, Paul
NIEMANN, Erich
ORTMANN, Walter
OTROMKE, Walter
OTTO, Gustav
PATZ, Johannes
PATZKE, Bernhard
PATZKE, Gunther
PATZKE, Herbert
PAUL, Emil - *less than 1 year imprisonment*
PAULITZ, Albert – *executed*
PAULS, Johann – *executed*
PEIKOWSKI, Paul
PENTZ, Martin - *5 years imprisonment*
PETERS, Friedrich
PETERS, Fritz – *executed*
PETTKE, Johannes
PFISTER, Johann - *5 years imprisonment*
PFODT, (Forename unknown)
PICK, Bruno
PIENERT, Bruno
PLATZ, Arthur
PLICHT, Johann
PLUHM, Hermann
POCHERT, Otto
POMMER, Albert
PREUSS, Leo
RACH, Hans – *executed*
RAMELOW, Walter
RAPPEL, Walter
RATHKE, Rudolf
REDDER, Heinrich
REDDER, Willi
REDMANN, Klemens
REDUHN, Kurt - *10 years imprisonment*
REGER, Karl - *8 years imprisonment*
REHBOGEN, Johann – *trial abandoned 2018*
REIMANN, Fritz
REIMANN, Paul
REXIN, Otto
REXIN, Paul
RINGEL, Paul
RINGEWALD, Walter
ROHDE, Ernst
ROSENKRANZ, Friedman
RÖSKE, Bernhard
RUDNICK, Ernst
RUNGE, Johannes
RUSCH, Herbert
SALTEN. Paul
SCHALK, Alfred
SCHALT, Wilhelm
SCHARFETTER, Erich
SCHEFFKE, Herbert
SCHENK, Werner von
SCHILLING, Arthur
SCHMALZ, Erich
SCHMIDT, Gottlieb
SCHOLL, Benno
SCHOLL, Max
SCHNEIDER, Otto - *10 years imprisonment*
SCHÖNFELDT. Ernst
SCHÖNROCK, Paul
SCHOWE, Max - *8 years imprisonment*
SCHRAAGE, Alexander
SCHRÖDER, Bernhard
SCHRÖDER, Fritz
SCHRÖDER, Max
SCHUCH, Richard
SCHULZ, Albert
SCHULZ, Bruno
SCHULZ, Fritz
SCHULZ, Johann
SCHULZ, Max
SCHWARTZ, Albert

SCHWARTZ, Friedrich Johann – *executed*
SCHWARTZ, Hermann
SCHWARZ, Christof - *3 years imprisonment*
SEEWE, Max
SKIERKA-SCHIERER, Leo
SKROBLIN, Hermann
SOIKE, Erich
SPORER, Johann - *4 years imprisonment*
STABENAU, Otto
STAGE, Martin - *8 years imprisonment*
STAHL, Josef - *10 years imprisonment*
STAMPNIOK, Erich - *5 years imprisonment*
STOLZ, Paul
STÜRMER, Emil
TESSMER, Friedrich
TESSMER, Heinz
TETZLAPE, John
THENN, Emil
THIEL, Klemens
THULKE, Ernst - 5 years imprisonment
THUN, Erich - *life in prison*
TIMM, Richard - *4 years imprisonment*
TISSLER, Alfred - *5 years imprisonment*
TOLKSDORF, Hans – *acquitted*
TOPOLSKI, Friedrich
TÖPPER, Otto
TREICHLER, Bruno
UKELEY, Bruno
UMLAND, Alfred
VOGLER, Wilhelm - 15 years imprisonment
VOLLMAN, Bruno
WAGNER, Emil
WALL, Johannes - *5 years imprisonment*
WALLRATH, Johannes
WALTER, Friedrich
WANGLER, Walter
WANNINGER, Leopold
WANSEL, Hans
WANSERSKI, Kurt
WARMBIER, Rudolf
WARNER, Kurt
WECKMUELLER, Albert - *15 years imprisonment*
WEICHBRODT, Otto
WEISNER, Andreas
WEISS, Franz
WELKE, Otto - *10 years imprisonment*
WELLNITZ, Paul – *executed*
WENNHARDT, Josef - *8 years imprisonment*
WENZEL, Emil - *10 years imprisonment*
WERNER, Karl
WESSEL, Horst
WIENHOLDT, Gerhard
WIESNER, August
WILHELM, Kurt
WILMS, Gustav
WISNER, Heinz
WITT, Arthur
WITT, Willy - *10 years imprisonment*
WITTE, Erich
WOELLNITZ, Werner - *less than 1 year imprisonment*
WOHLFEIL, Richard - *less than 1 year imprisonment*
WOLF, Johann
WOLFE, Paul
WÖLMS, Hermann
WÖLMS, Willi
WOLTER, Adalbert - *8 years imprisonment*
WORM, Arthur

WROBEL, Johann - *less than 1 year imprisonment*
WULE, Ernst
ZIEHM, Hugo - *3 years imprisonment*
ZIELINSKI, Johann
ZIEMANN, Bruno
ZIEMENS, Gustav
ZERLIN, Eduard - *12 years imprisonment*
ZUBE, Kurt
ZURELL, Karl – *executed*
ZWINGMANN, Franz

Kapos

KOPCZYNSKI, Tadeusz – *hanged*
KOWALSKI, Kazimierz - *3 years imprisonment*
KOZLOWSKI, Waclaw – *hanged*
NIKOLAYSEN, Alfred – *executed*
REITER, Josef – *hanged*
SPILLMAN, Franz – *acquitted*
SZOPINSKI, Fanciszek – *hanged*

Female Guards

BANKEWITZ, Christel
BARKMANN, Jenny Wanda – *hanged 1946*
BAUM, Irene
BECKER, Elisabeth– *hanged*
BECKER, Ria Jorink
BEILHARDT, Erna - 5 years imprisonment
BORN, Elisabeth
BOSCH, Anni (born 1904) - 3 years imprisonment
BOTHE, Herta - 5 years imprisonment
DASE, Lydia
DEMANGET, Erna
EKRUTT, Auguste
FREIGEN, Charlotte
GLAW, Anneliese
HANSEN, Elfriede
HARTJES, Gertrud
HEINEN, Nelly
HOLINSKI, Ursela
JOBSEN, Emma
KATCHEN, Margarethe
KATSCHER, Ursula
KERST, Frieda
KLAFF, Wanda – *hanged 1946*
KLEIN, Charlotte
KOPP, Anna *(born 1904)*
KOSKE, Gertrud
KRANZ, Erna
KREUSZ, Helene *(born 1904)*
KRISCHEWSKI, Martha
KRUEGER, Erna
KUNATH, Gerda
LEHMANN, Lilli
LENZ, Hildegard
LICKFERS, Jenny *(born 1920)*
LUTH, Elisabeth
PICKHOLTZ, Olga Barnitsch
MARQUARDT, Emmy
MULLER, Liselotte
NAUMANN, Erna
OBERAUF, Lieselotte
OKON, Margarete
PARADIES, Ewa – *hanged 1946*
PILS, Maria Pils
RATTMANN, Erna
RHEINHOLT, Gertrud
RODE, Ilse
ROPER, Magalena
ROSE, Maria
SASS, Ilse
SCHAARSCHMIDT, Paula
SCHARBERT, Anna
SCHMIDT, Anne Lotte
SCHULZ, Martha
SCHULZ, Erika *(born 1907) - 7 years imprisonment*
SCHULT, Pauline Franziska *(born 1892)*
STEINHOFF, Gerda – *hanged 1946*

STIEGLER, Charlotte
STOWER, Christel
SUESS, Rosy
THEWS, Edith
THIMM, Elisabeth
VESPER, Gertrud
WENZEL, Kathe
ZIEGLER, Hildegard
WILL, Edith
WISCH, Sofie
WISOTZKI, Johanna
WOLLWEBER, Erna
ZAGST, Else
ZIEGLER, Else

APPENDIX II
STUTTHOF WAR CRIMES VERDICTS

Verdicts from 1st Gdańsk War Crimes Trial

BARKMANN, Jenny-Wanda, *SS Aufseherin*: sentenced to death, executed: July 4, 1946
BECKER, Elisabeth, *SS Aufseherin*: sentenced to death, executed: July 4, 1946
BEILHARDT, Erna, *SS-Aufseherin*: sentenced to 5 years imprisonment
BREIT, Jan, *SS Aufseherin*: sentenced to death, executed: July 4, 1946
KLAFF, Wanda, *SS Aufseherin*: sentenced to death, executed: July 4, 1946
KOPCZYNSKI, Tadeusz, *Kapo*: sentenced to death, executed: July 4, 1946
KOWALSKI, Kazimierz, *Kapo*: sentenced to 3 years imprisonment
KOZLOWSKI, Waclaw, *Kapo*: sentenced to death, executed: July 4, 1946
PARADIES, Ewa, sentenced to death, executed: July 4, 1946
PAULS, Johann, *SS-Oberscharführer*: sentenced to death, executed: July 4, 1946
REITER, Josef, *Kapo*: sentenced to death, executed: July 4, 1946
STEINHOFF, Gerda, *SS Blockleiterin*: sentenced to death, executed: July 4, 1946
SZOPINSKI, Fanciszek, *Kapo*: sentenced to death, executed: July 4, 1946

Verdicts from 2nd Gdańsk war Crimes Trial

DIETRICH, Kurt, *SS Unterscharführer*: sentenced to death, executed: October 10, 1947
EGGERT, Karl, *SS Rottenführer*: sentenced to death, executed: October 10, 1947
ENGLERT, Walter, *SS Scharführer*: 3 years imprisonment
FOTH, Ewald, *SS Oberscharführer*:: sentenced to death, executed: October 10, 1947
GÖRTZ, Johannes, *SS Unterscharführer*: 8 years imprisonment
GOTTCHAU, Oskar, *SS Unterscharführer*: 10 years imprisonment
GRAMS, Adolf, *SS Rottenführer*: 10 years imprisonment
MEYER, Theodor, *SS Hauptsturmführer*: sentenced to death, executed: October 10, 1947
NIKOLAYSEN, Alfred, *Kapo*: sentenced to death, executed: October 10, 1947
PAULITZ, Albert, *SS Oberscharführer*: sentenced to death, executed: October 10, 1947
PETERS, Fritz, *SS Unterscharführer*: sentenced to death, executed: October 10, 1947
RACH, Hans, *SS Oberscharführer*: sentenced to death, executed: October 10, 1947
REGER, Karl, *SS Scharführer*:: 8 years imprisonment
STAGE, Martin, *SS Scharführer*: 8 years imprisonment
THUN, Erich, *SS Unterscharführer*: life imprisonment

VOGLER, Wilhelm, *SS Hauptsturmführer*: 15 years imprisonment
WELLNITZ, Paul, *SS Rottenführer*: sentenced to death, executed: October 10, 1947
WENNHARDT, Josef, *SS Scharführer*: 8 years imprisonment
WENZEL, Emil, *SS Unterscharführer*: 10 years imprisonment
WÖLLNITZ, Werner, *SS Rottenführer*: 10 years imprisonment
WOLTER, Adalbert, *SS Unterscharführer*: 8 years imprisonment
ZERLIN, Eduard, *SS Unterscharführer*:: 12 years imprisonment
ZIEHM, Hugo, *SS Scharführer*: 3 years imprisonment
ZURELL, Karl, *SS Rottenführer*: sentenced to death, executed: October 10, 1947

Verdicts from 3rd Gdańsk War Crimes Trial

DIRNBERGER, Nikolaus, *SS Scharführer*: 4 years imprisonment
EBERLE, Gustav, *SS Hauptscharführer*: 10 years imprisonment
JASSEN, Erich, *SS Hauptscharführer*: 10 years imprisonment
KLAFFKE, Adolf, *SS Oberscharführer*: 10 years imprisonment
KLAWAN, Nikolai, *SS Scharführer*: 3 years imprisonment
LICHTNER, Johann, *SS Hauptscharführer*: 5 years imprisonment
LÖWEN, Heinz, *SS Scharführer*: 5 years imprisonment
MEINCK, Karl, *SS Obersturmführer*: 12 years imprisonment
MÖHRKE, Hans, *SS Sturmscharführer*: 4 years imprisonment
MÜLLER, Harry, *SS Unterscharführer*: 4 years imprisonment
SCHNEIDER, Otto, *SS Unterscharführer*: 10 years imprisonment
SPORER, Johann, *SS Unterscharführer*: 4 years imprisonment
STAMPNIOK, Erich, *SS Unterscharführer*: 5 years imprisonment
TESSMER, Friedrich, *SS Scharführer*: 4 years imprisonment
THULKE, Ernst, *SS Rottenführer*: 5 years imprisonment
TIMM, Richard, *SS Hauptscharführer*: 4 years imprisonment
TISSLER, Alfred, *SS Rottenführer*: 5 years imprisonment
TOKSDORF, Hans, *SS Oberscharführer*: acquitted and released
WELKE, Otto, *SS Sturmscharführer*: 10 years imprisonment
WITT, Willy, *SS Unterscharführer*: 10 years imprisonment

Verdicts from 4th Gdańsk War Crimes Trial

AKOLT, Richard, *SS Rottenführer*: 3 years imprisonment
BAUMGARTNER, Leopold, *SS Oberscharführer*: 7 months imprisonment
BERG, Rudolf, *SS Scharführer*: 10 years imprisonment
BRODOWSKI, Gustav, *SS Rottenführer*: 7 months imprisonment
BUTH, Willi, *SS Hauptscharführer*: life imprisonment
ECKERMANN, Bernard, *SS Oberscharführer*: 7 months imprisonment
GLAWE, Fritz, *SS Unterscharführer*: 10 years imprisonment
HENKE, Waldemar, *SS Obersturmführer*: 5 years imprisonment
KAUTZ, Gustav, *SS Unterscharführer*: 5 years imprisonment
KNAPPERT, Ernst, *SS Rottenführer*: 7 months imprisonment

KNIFFKE, Anton, *SS Scharführer*: 3 years imprisonment
KÖPKE, Horst, *SS Unterscharführer*: 10 years imprisonment
LASCHEIT, Emil, *SS Sturmscharführer*: 10 years imprisonment
LINK, Hermann, *SS Scharführer*: 5 years imprisonment
MERTENS, Erich, *SS Oberscharführer*: 5 years imprisonment
PAUL, Emil, *SS Unterscharführer*: 7 months imprisonment
PENTZ, Martin, *SS Scharführer*: 5 years imprisonment
PFISTER, Johann, *SS Rottenführer*: 5 years imprisonment
REDUHN, Kurt, *SS Unterscharführer*: 10 years imprisonment
RINGEWALD, Walter, *SS Oberscharführer*: 7 months imprisonment
SCHWARZ, Christof, *SS Hauptsturmführer*: 3 years imprisonment
SPILLMAN, Franz, *Kapo*: acquitted
STAHL, Josef, *SS Unterscharführer*: 10 years imprisonment
WALL, Johannes, *SS Sturmscharführer*: 5 years imprisonment
WECKMÜLLER, Albert, *SS Hauptsturmführer*: 15 years imprisonment
WOHLFEIL, Richard, *SS Hauptscharführer*: 7 months imprisonment
WROBEL, Johann, *SS Oberscharführer*: 7 months imprisonment

Verdict from Torun War Crimes Trial

JACOBI, Hans, *SS-Hauptsturmführer*, 3 years imprisonment

Verdict from final Gdańsk War Crimes Trial

BIELWA, Paul, *Rottenführer* 12 years imprisonment

SELECT ENGLISH BIBLIOGRAPHY

ALLEN, Michael Thad: *The Business of Genocide: The SS, Slave Labor, and the Concentration Camps.* (2002 Chapel Hill: University of North Carolina Press)

BALDWIN, Josh: *Trawniki Guards – Foot Soldiers Of The Holocaust* (2020 Schiffer Military)

BANNISTER, Sybil: *I Lived Under Hitler* (1995 Penguin)

BLATMAN, Daniel: *Death Marches: The Final Phase of Nazi Genocide* (2011 Belknap Harvard)

BROWN, Daniel Patrick: *The Camp Women – The Female Auxiliaries Who Assisted In Running The Nazi Concentration Camp System* (2002 Schiffer Military History)

CIEŚLAK, Edmund and BIERNAT, Czesław: *History of Gdańsk* (1995 Fundacji Biblioteki Gdańskiej)

DEBSKI, TADEUSZ: *A Battlefield Of Ideas – Nazi Concentration Camps and Their Polish Prisoners* (2001 Columbia University Press)

DRZYCIMSKI, Andrzej and GORSKI, Janusz: *The Redoubt Westerplatte* (2015 Oficyna Gdańska)

FULLBROOK, Mary: *Reckonings* (2018 Oxford University Press)

GELLATELY, Robert and STOLTZ, Nathan: *Social Outsiders In Nazi Germany* (2001 Princeton University Press)

GILBERT, Martin: *The Holocaust* (1987 Fontana)

GOLDHAGEN, Daniel Jionah: *Hitler's Willing Executioners – Ordinary Germans and The Holocaust* (1996 Little, Brown & Company)

GRABOWSKA-CHALKA, Janina: *Stutthof Guide - Historical Information* (2011 Muzeum Stutthof)

GRAF, Jurgen and MATTOGNO, Carlo: *Concentration Camp Stutthoff: Its History and Function In National Socialist Jewish Policy* (2015 Castle Hill Publishers)

HALTER, Roman: *Roman's Journey* (2012 Arcade)

HARGREAVES, Richard: *Blitkreig Unleashed: The German Invasion of Poland 1939* (2008 Pen and Sword Books)

HELM, Sarah: *If This Is A Woman* (2015 Abacus)

JØRGENSEN, Tore: *Stutthof Diaries Collection: For Truth & Honor* (2022 Friesen Press)

KAMPINSKI, Marian: *Remember Me: A Holocaust Survivor's Story* (2009 iUniverse)

KAY, Alex J. and STAHEL, David: *Mass Violence In Nazi-Occuped Europe* (2018 Indiana University Press)

KOVALA, Liisa: *Surviving Stutthof: My Father's Memories Behind The Death Gate* (2017 Latitude 46 Publishing)

LEVINE, Herbert S: *Hitler's Free City: A History of the Nazi Party In Danzig 1925-1939* (1973 The University of Chicago Press)

LEWIS, Helen: *A Time To Speak* (2010 Blackstaff Press)

LONGERICH, Peter: *The Unwritten Order: Hitler's Role In The Final Solution* (2001 The History Press)

LOWER, Wendy: *Hitler's Furies: German Women In The Nazi Killing Fields* (2014 Vintage)

MALAK, Father Henryk Maria: *Shavelings In Death Camps – A Polish Priest's Memoir Of Imprisonment By The Nazis 1939-1945* (2012 McFarland & Company)

MAZOWER, Mark: *Hitler's Empire – Nazi Rule In Occupied Europe* (2008 Allen Lane)

MCDONOUGH, Frank: *The Gestapo: The Myths and Reality of Hitler's Secret Police* (2015 Coronet)

McNAMARA, Paul: *Sean Lester, Poland and The Nazi Takeover of Danzig* (2009 Irish Academic Press)

MEISEL, Phillip: *The Keeper Of Miracles* (2021 MacMillan Australia)

MICHAELIS, Rolf: *SS-Heimwehr Danzig In Poland 1939* (2008 Schiffer Publishing)

ORSKI, Marek: *The Extermination Of The Stutthof Concentration Camp Prisoners Using The Poisonous Cyclone B Gas* (available online)

ORSKI, Marek: *The Last Days of Stutthof* (available online)

PITT, Ingrid: *Darkness Before the Dawn* (2013 Hemlock Press)

REITLINGER, Gerald: *The SS: Alibi Of A Nation 1922-1945* (1981 Arms & Armour Press)

ROLNIKAITE, Maria: *I Must Tell* (2018 Lulu.com)

SCHMIDT, Hermine: *Unfettered Joy* (2005 Gramma)

SRUOGA, Balys: *Forest Of The Gods* (1996 Vaga)

SCHWERTFEGER, Professor Ruth: *A Nazi Camp Near Danzig: Perspectives On Shame And On The Holocaust From Stutthof* (2022 Bloomsbury Academic)

STRAEDE, Prof. Therkel; OVERBY, Martin Jensen; MÜLLER, Dr. Reiner: *Stutthof Maritime Evacuations Project – Academic Report* (2021 International Holocause Remembrance Alliance)

TIGHE, Carl: *National Identity In The Polish-German Borderlands* (1990 PlutoPress)

WACHMANN, Nikolaus: *KL: A History of the Nazi Concentration Camps* (2015 Abacus)

WEALE, Adrian: *The SS: A New History* (2010 Abacus)

WAEALE, Adrian: *Renegades – Hitler's Englishmen* (1994 Weidenfeld & Nicolson)

WEINBERG, Jeshajahu and ELIELI, Rina: *The Holocaust Memorial In Washington* (1995 Rizzoli International Publications)

WILLIAMS, A.T.: *A Passing Fury – Searching For Justice At The End Of World War II* (2016 Vintage)

WILM, Leo: *Memories Of The Waffen SS* (2017 Schiffer Publishing)

WINSTONE,Martin: *The Dark Heart Of Hitler's Europe* (2015 IB Taurus)

YLA, Stasys: *A Priest In Stutthof – Human Experiences In The World of The Subhuman* (1971 Manyland Books)

ZILBER, Ettie: *A Holocaust Memoir Of Love & Resilence* (2019 Amsterdam Publishers)

INDEX

My grateful thanks for all the assistance given by staff of the Stutthof Museum, as well as the Museum of the Second World War, the Post Office Museum and the Jewish Theatre (all in Gdansk) and to Joanna Leszczynska who first took me to see a concentration camp so little known to English-speaking scholars that in the index at the back of almost any textbook on the war, the concentration camp system, the Holocaust and the Third Reich, it rates no more than a bare mention, and only too commonly not even that.

And as always with such books as this, any mistakes of factual misunderstanding or translation are the author's responsibility and if notified will be corrected in future editions. Likewise any misattribution of any photograph used.

Andrew Sparke

Printed in Great Britain
by Amazon

27210348R00155